What's that
Bird?

What's that Bird?

A starter's guide to birds of southern Africa

Kenneth Newman

Dedicated to all starter birders

Struik Publishers
(a division of New Holland Publishing South Africa (Pty) Ltd)
Cornelis Struik House
80 McKenzie Street
Cape Town 8001
New Holland Publishing is a member of the
Johnnic Publishing Group.

Visit us at **www.struik.co.za**
Log on to our photographic website **www.imagesofafrica.co.za** for an African experience.

First published in 2003
1 3 5 7 9 10 8 6 4 2

Publishing manager: Pippa Parker
Managing editor: Helen de Villiers
Editor: Jeanne Hromnik
Design director: Janice Evans
Designer: Robin Cox
Proofreader: Tessa Kennedy

Reproduction by Hirt & Carter Cape (Pty) Ltd
Printed and bound by Sirivatana Interprint Public Co Ltd

ISBN 1 86872 879 X

Front cover (top): Like all cranes, Grey Crowned Cranes are gregarious
when not breeding. (Photo: Roger de la Harpe)
Front cover (centre): A yellow weaver (the male Masked Weaver)
in breeding plumage. (Photo: Gerald Hinde)
Page 3: The birder's boast – the Narina Trogon – in its forest habitat. (Photo: Hugh Chittenden)

A word from the author

Anyone wishing to get to know southern Africa's birds may be excused for feeling a little daunted. Our bird books confront the reader with a dazzling but, at first, confusing array of avian creatures – brown ones, green ones, grey ones, yellow ones, many looking very much the same. Making sense of them, and ultimately coming to recognize them all, may at first seem an impossible task. But it need not be, and the key to unlocking the bewildering world of birds lies in this book.

Individual birds (i.e. species) all belong to larger groups and are part of them because they share common features, be they physical similarities or habitats or territories. By coming to terms with the various groups of birds in this book – a manageable 60 or so – you can easily enter the greater world of birds and begin the task of identifying specific birds by first identifying the group to which they most probably belong.

The groups and species described here have been chosen to provide you, the Starter, with easily found and identifiable birds that you can locate without much trouble. Many are birds that you will see (or will already have seen) near your home or in day-to-day travelling. Some, however, live in particular habitats and must be looked for there. For the most part, the groups presented here follow family groupings, but sometimes it has been more useful to group birds that are easily confused with one another, or that share a habitat such as water.

Once you are familiar with the more common groups and species in the broad habitat divisions in which they have been arranged here, you will be able to progress with confidence to the more difficult groups (the numerous little brown birds, seabirds, shorebirds and birds of prey), which are handled in a separate section at the end of the book. When you reach this point, there will be no holding you back.

I strongly recommend using this book in conjunction with a field-guide such as *Newman's Birds of Southern Africa*. This will help you become familiar with more birds in their various groups and will introduce you at the same time to the fieldguide concept and how it works.

Most of us want to become proficient quickly in any new sphere we enter, but when it come to identifying birds, speed can soon bring on a bout of ornithological indigestion. Birding, at all times, should be pleasurable, relaxing. If it becomes a chore, give it a rest. Eventually, it will take you to new and pleasant places that you didn't know existed. You will make new friends and gain a new purpose in life. It can be an absorbing interest. But don't rush it.

Kenneth Newman

Easily recognized, the world's largest bird hardly requires an introduction.

Contents

Grasslands & drylands

Seashores & estuaries

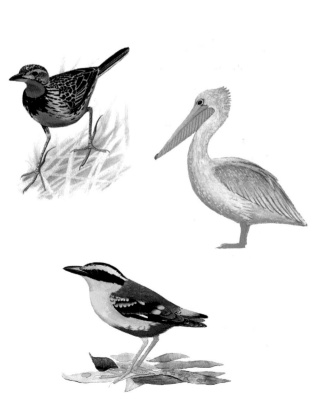

Introduction

Birding – the pursuit of finding and identifying birds – is one of the fastest growing pursuits and attracts people of all ages and from all walks of life. A fieldguide to the birds of a particular region is the common – and essential – tool needed for birding. But how do you begin in a region such as ours, which boasts more than 900 bird species spread through a guide of more than 400 pages? The secret lies in this book, *A Starter's Guide*, which aims to make your entry into birding much simpler. You will be introduced to different groups of birds and to the more common species within the group, and are encouraged to familiarize yourself with the *group* before you try to commit to memory individual species.

Most people 'know' a few birds without realizing it – for instance, the noisy Hadeda Ibis or the Egyptian Goose. Anyone with a garden will probably recognize at least one bulbul and will have seen a weaver, wagtail, starling or sparrow without having paid any particular attention. Next time you see one of these birds, stop and take a second look. You probably have a 'life list' (a birding term for a list of all species seen) of six or eight birds already.

The Cape Glossy Starling is easily recognized as a starling by its swaggering walk and glossy plumage. It is a common town bird, also found in many other habitats.

Watch thrushes, for instance, as they run or hop about (they use both forms of locomotion) and become familiar with their appearance and behaviour as they forage for worms. Also watch for the European Starling or Common Mynah and compare them with the thrushes. All are of similar size, but their behaviours are quite different and are shared by members of their respective families. Once this fact is grasped, you will be able to identify other thrushes or starlings, at least by family, when you encounter them. The same applies, obviously, to all other bird groups.

For the purposes of this book, family has usually been used as the basis of grouping, with the focus on groups that are easy to recognize and on the most commonly seen species in the group. In some instances, however, unrelated but similar-looking birds have been grouped. Further, where birds share a common habitat, as in the case of flamingoes and the Hamerkop, which almost invariably are seen together at fresh water, the grouping is based on shared habitat.

The reader is encouraged to start in familiar territory – a back garden or local park – and to venture out from there, having mastered the commonly seen town and city groups of birds. A bird sanctuary is the next obvious step. Most of these have a water feature of some kind, a small dam or lake that will provide an interesting variety of waterbirds. The water environment with its attendant birds will help top up the list of groups you can easily recognize, and from here on you will be able to look more generally and further afield.

Before long, you will be ready to progress to the 'More difficult to identify' bird groups and those birds that are 'More difficult to find' – described at the end of the book. You will also find that you are able to understand and use a bird fieldguide with ease.

The various bird groups in this book have been arranged loosely according to their appearance in broad habitat or vegetation zones: urban areas (including parks and gardens); inland waters; woodlands and bush; grasslands and drylands; seashores and estuaries. Bear in mind that these groupings are not mutually exclusive and many birds will naturally occur in more than one or even two of the habitats/zones in which they are presented here. However, these broad divisions provide the Starter with useful clusters and will help make sense quickly and easily of what can be a bewildering range of birds.

WHAT IS A FAMILY?

All birds (or other living things, for that matter) are grouped in families. Ducks and geese, for instance, are one family (Anatidae). Families are divided into genera and genera into species, each of which differs from all other species in some way. Normally, members of a species can reproduce only with those of the same species. This comes about through discrete courtship rituals in different species, including both physical displays and voice.

All species have two scientific names: the first the genus, the second the species or specific name. For example, the common House Sparrow is known as *Passer domesticus*. *Passer* (always with a capital first letter) is the genus; *domesticus* is the specific (personal) name. Every other species in the genus *Passer* has its own, unique, name. The Egyptian Goose is the only species in its genus – *Alopochen*.

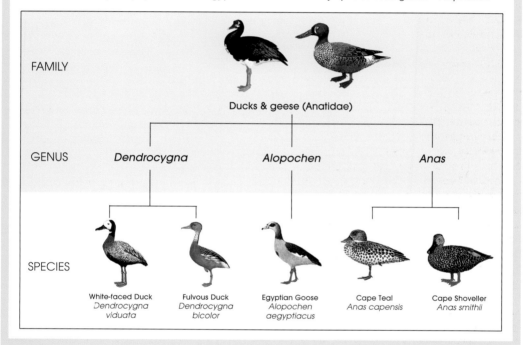

FAMILY

Ducks & geese (Anatidae)

GENUS   *Dendrocygna*   *Alopochen*   *Anas*

SPECIES

| White-faced Duck *Dendrocygna viduata* | Fulvous Duck *Dendrocygna bicolor* | Egyptian Goose *Alopochen aegyptiacus* | Cape Teal *Anas capensis* | Cape Shoveller *Anas smithii* |

Starting on home ground

The best place for a starter birder is the garden, if you have one. In even the smallest gardens there are a dozen or so birds that visit regularly; larger gardens may attract as many as 30 species in any month. The local park is often a good substitute for a garden, especially if there happens to be a water feature.

Even when you can identify the birds in your garden and in the area, it is always entertaining to see them up close and on a regular basis. Food is a good way to make this happen, and often tempts new species that appear unheralded. Establish a feeding station within a few metres of a window from which you can watch easily. The term sounds a bit grand, but need only be an old tray suspended from a tree.

Alternatively, buy a bird feeder from a pet shop or hardware store. It is a good idea to buy a small seed-feeder as well so that the usual hordes of sparrows and doves can feed separately from fruit- and insect-eaters. This way your offerings of fruit will last longer. The feeding station should be placed no closer than four metres from the window or the birds will be disturbed by movements in the house. It is useful to keep a pair of binoculars nearby.

There is no need to supply seed-eaters with anything more costly than crushed maize meal. Meal for small chickens is adequate, most seed-eaters being themselves small. All birds eat bread and will feast on crusts or stale slices dampened under the tap. Barbets, bulbuls, go-away birds, thrushes and other fruit-eaters obviously prefer soft fruits, pawpaw skins, apples and the like. Impale the fruit on an

W. Tarboton

A Crested Barbet at a 'feeding station'.

upward-projecting nail to prevent more vigorous consumers knocking it to the ground, and take care to hang your feeder beyond the reach of pets. While crushing grain with their bills, seed-eaters drop a lot of it on the ground, which is where the doves feed. Get to know doves. Two or three species will probably come to your feeder.

It is a good idea to feed 'your' birds at a regular time daily, the earlier in the day the better. (They tend to gather expectantly.) Birds are at their most active in the morning from dawn to about 11:00 and again from about 16:00 until nightfall. In the middle of the day, most birds tend to seek shade and to rest. Of course there are exceptions. Sunbirds, for example, seem to feed tirelessly all day when nectar-bearing flowers are in blossom. Place your feeding station in the shade if possible, close to a leafy bush. This will prevent the food from drying in the sun and will also give the birds a handy escape route from real or perceived dangers.

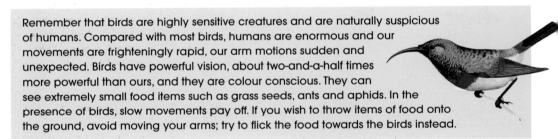

Remember that birds are highly sensitive creatures and are naturally suspicious of humans. Compared with most birds, humans are enormous and our movements are frighteningly rapid, our arm motions sudden and unexpected. Birds have powerful vision, about two-and-a-half times more powerful than ours, and they are colour conscious. They can see extremely small food items such as grass seeds, ants and aphids. In the presence of birds, slow movements pay off. If you wish to throw items of food onto the ground, avoid moving your arms; try to flick the food towards the birds instead.

Exploring local wetlands

Once you have assembled a list of 20 to 30 birds that you know with confidence, you will want to move on to a bird sanctuary (preferably one with a viewing hide) or a wetland where you will be able to see large numbers of birds. These are lonely places, however, and you are well advised to keep your watch or cell-phone concealed and to take whatever safety precautions you can. Most districts have at least one or two wetlands that can be visited, although permission is usually required if they are located on private land.

Your local sewage disposal plant is a wetland that is well worth checking out, and permission to enter with a car is usually given. Your interest in this location may cause raised eyebrows, but sewage plants are in fact very productive locations. Once the waste has been treated, the water is pumped into a series of man-made settlement pans that attract numerous

Flocks of flamingoes and – a less familiar sight – a lakeside assembly of Great White Pelicans.

Shrike

Starling

Robin-chat

Thrush

Dabbling duck

Whistling duck

RECOGNIZING JIZZ

The general impression a bird makes on you when you first see it is known as its jizz. The common Cattle Egret, for example, is unmistakably a heron not merely because of its long legs and longish neck (other bird families share these features) but because of its distinctive posture. Likewise, we know that a bird with a particular strut and bobbing tail must be a wagtail. There are 13 different starlings and they all have a distinctive family jizz. So do all sunbirds, bee-eaters and woodpeckers, among others.

The importance of recognizing the jizz of different bird groups early in the game cannot be stressed too strongly. Look carefully at the 13 southern African robins in the pages of your fieldguide. They share not only body shape and size but postures such as the perky way in which they perch and their tail-up stance.

Note how most ducks stand with their bodies in the horizontal position. They waddle as they walk because their legs are widely spaced and are placed in the middle of the body. No other waterbird walks in this fashion. Whistling ducks have a different jizz, however. They have an erect goose-like stance and walk without waddling.

waterbirds and other birds associated with wet or swampy conditions. The other advantage of a sewage farm is that most of your bird viewing can be done from the car, itself an ideal hide.

The range of birds to be seen at a wetland depends very much on its location. Gulls are often in residence near the coast, the Grey-headed Gull being also an inland breeder. Gulls present their own ID problems, especially if young birds are there. Take your time, try to place each bird species in a family, and write notes for later reference. If the number of birds is confusing, concentrate on three or four species; the others will probably still be there on your next visit.

Watch the open water for ducks, geese, cormorants, moorhens, coots and dabchicks. On the shoreline, plovers and other small shorebirds may be probing in the shallows or the mud, particularly in summer. The Three-banded Plover, common at wetlands, is quite colourful. The elegant Black-Winged Stilt and the Avocet may also be there. Watch out too for wagtails and the Blacksmith Plover. Ignore nondescript species for the moment and look for larger birds. Herons (both the Grey Heron and Little Egret) could be present and are relatively easy to identify. Reedbeds are also a hive of activity especially when weavers, bishops and others are coming and going in summer.

It is important to approach waterbirds with minimum disturbance or they will flush and leave you looking at an expanse of open water. If possible, drive up slowly and park in a good viewing spot. Try not to bang car doors. If you are lucky enough to be in easy reach of a proclaimed bird sanctuary, you may be able to watch from a viewing hide with a screened approach. Do enter the hide quietly and close the door since other birders may be there already. There is nothing quite so embarrassing as sitting down with a tantalizing view of dozens of waterbirds and hearing the door blow shut behind you with a bang!

Venturing further afield into diverse habitats

About 16 different habitats can be distinguished in southern Africa, each with its associated bird species. Commercial **plantations** may be considered a habitat, but these man-made forests of exotic trees grown for timber are avifaunal deserts. Little sun penetrates and there is no ground cover, the trees closely planted for rapid growth. However, buzzards, doves and canaries may sometimes be seen on the fringes of plantations.

Woodlands and bush

Francolins, hornbills, flycatchers, shrikes, woodpeckers, barbets, go-away birds, nightjars, kingfishers, ground thrushes, cuckoos, honey-guides, korhaans and many raptors are at home in **woodlands**. The medium-high trees that form this habitat are spaced such that their canopies do not interlock and sunlight can penetrate, encouraging growth of a good grassy ground cover. Woodlands may be 'moist' or 'dry' according to altitude and soil type. They are also labelled according to the dominant vegetation, such as mopane or burkea trees.

The mixed woodland habitat of bushveld.

A number of specialists such as the White Cuckooshrike, Blue-spotted Dove, Thick-billed Cuckoo, Golden-backed Pytilia, Rufous-bellied Tit and Miombo Rock Thrush live in miombo woodland, which is dominated by broad-leaved trees of the *Brachystegia spiciformis* (msasa) and *Julbernardia globiflora* (munondo) species and occurs only in Zimbabwe and some central African countries. Tree canopies are almost closed – unusual in woodland – but more open than in true forest. Dappled sunlight penetrates, but the ground cover is limited. Insectivorous and frugivorous birds are more numerous in the evergreen swaths formed by riparian or riverine woodland than in the surrounding dry, deciduous bush.

Among the rich array of **bushveld** birds are the birds that are generally found in woodlands as well as sunbirds, robins, helmet shrikes, guineafowls, weavers, vultures, storks, coursers, nightjars, bustards, larks and most warblers. This is a mixed-tree biome where canopies touch at mid-level. Most of the trees are of medium height and they are usually interspersed with bushes, either broad-leaved or thorn.

An especially large number of small birds, including flycatchers, sunbirds, waxbills, tits, titbabblers, crombeks, weavers, larks and a host of warblers, are found in **thornveld**. As the name suggests, this is a woodland type comprised of small thorn trees, which is often found on sandy soils.

Storks, eagles, accipiters, bustards, korhaans, vultures, hornbills, woodpeckers, francolins, coursers and plovers are found in **mature thorn savanna** along with most of the birds that occur in thornveld.

Evergreen forests house some spectacular birds, but are a difficult habitat for birders.

Thorn savanna comprises a mosaic of both large and small trees grouped on Kalahari sands. Thorn trees dominate and there is a rich ground cover. Trees are mostly grouped, with grassy areas between.

Certain robin-chats, bush shrikes, the Knysna Turaco, Narina Trogon, Square-tailed Drongo, Cape Batis, Dusky and Blue-mantled flycatchers, Cape Parrot, Grey Cuckooshrike, Crowned Eagle, forest bulbuls, forest doves and the Buff-spotted Flufftail are found in **evergreen forest**, a specialized habitat in the high rainfall regions of the eastern escarpment and the coastal regions of the Eastern Cape and KwaZulu-Natal. Birding in such forests requires determination and patience as many birds are found high in the dense canopy, but it is very rewarding.

Many regular evergreen forest species as well as a number of local species, such as the Red-fronted Tinkerbird, Rudd's Apalis, Scaly-throated Honeyguide, Wattle-eyed Flycatcher and Southern Banded Snake Eagle, are found in **dune forests**, the mature evergreen forest that occurs locally on the coastal littoral in KwaZulu-Natal. Many small birds, including the White-browed Scrub Robin, Crimson-breasted Boubou, Black-crowned Tchagra, Blue Waxbill, Melba Finch and Green-backed Bleating Warbler, prefer the dense, tangled bush and associated rank grass of **thickets**, often found on termite mounds.

Grasslands and drylands

A wide variety of korhaans, larks, pipits, coursers, francolins and cranes are found in **grasslands**, a habitat that is shrinking fast as a result of urban spread, highways and farming. Ground Woodpeckers, Sickle-winged Chats, Gurney's Sugarbirds and francolins are found in mountain grassland, a habitat much reduced by the spread of exotic timber plantations. The Blue Swallow is a summer breeder in isolated locations, mostly at high altitude in the mistbelt of the Drakensberg and to the north. Montane grassland slopes are strewn with rocks and protea trees, and pockets of evergreen forest grow in the kloofs.

Larks, korhaans, warblers and canaries as well as raptors, including Black and Martial eagles and kestrels, inhabit **karoo** in the semi-arid south-central and west-central parts of southern Africa. The flat or undulating stony plains of this habitat are sparsely dotted with succulent plants, shrubs and small trees. Annual rainfall is 150–300 mm but may be as little as 50–200 mm in the more arid areas, where desert grasses predominate.

The Pale Chanting Goshawk, Greater Kestrel, Black Crow, Red-eyed Bulbul, Capped Wheatear, Marico Flycatcher, Northern Black Korhaan and Double-banded Courser are the resident species that are most in evidence in **semi-desert**, typified by the tree and bush savanna of the central Kalahari in Botswana. This habitat is home to a surprisingly wide variety of birds, residents as well as seasonal summer visitors such as Red-backed and Lesser Grey shrikes, Caspian Plovers and various migrant warblers. A number of korhaan, lark and chat species are – surprisingly – found in the flat, stony plains and dunes of **desert**, a habitat typical of Namibia. The rivers that flow infrequently through these inhospitable parts support trees, their roots deep in underground water. They provide a home for many birds, including starlings, barbets and hornbills.

A number of endemic species, including Victorin's Warbler, Cape Sugarbird, Protea Canary, Orange-breasted Sunbird and others are at home in **fynbos**. This rich endemic scrubland is found in the rocky, mountainous regions of the Western Cape, extending to Port Elizabeth. It is composed of proteas, small-leaved heaths and reed-like restios.

G. Dreyer/SIL

Restios and proteas in a patch of fynbos.

Seashores and estuaries

A rich fauna of small birds, most of them difficult to see, inhabit **coastal bush**, a type of dense coastal forest stunted by salt-laden off-sea winds. It supports a mixed vegetation in which the banana-like leaves of *Strelitzia* are conspicuous. Watch for interesting species such as turacos, hornbills and barbets. Tambourine Doves fly out occasionally and Black Saw-winged Swallows are quite often in evidence. River **estuaries** are often full of pleasant surprises and splendid waterbird gatherings are to be found on both east and south-east coasts, fresh- and salt-water birds congregating on the sandbanks. In addition to the various herons and gulls, there may be storks, the African Black Oystercatcher, flamingoes, pelicans and terns, even a Fish Eagle. The Mangrove Kingfisher is a bird to look out for in **mangrove swamp**, a threatened habitat confined to small pockets on the east and north-east coasts.

ANATOMY 0F A BIRD

It is necessary to know the names of the various parts of a bird if you are to understand the descriptions, however simple, in fieldguides. You may wonder why, for instance, the White-fronted Bee-eater is so called when it obviously does not have a white breast. If you check the anatomy diagram below, you will see that the 'front' of a bird is not its chest but the front of its forehead. Likewise, you might be interested in where exactly secondaries, primaries and coverts are located – or tarsus or moustachial-stripe. Birds have eye-rings, eyebrows, eye-stripes and rictal bristles, and their nails are at the tips of their beaks.

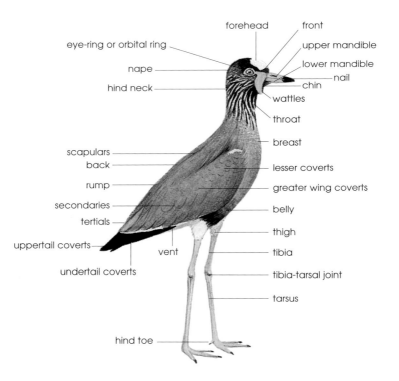

The main feathers on a bird's wing are the flight feathers. They consist of outer primary (the most important feathers, which may be likened to the fingers of a human hand) and secondary feathers, and the small bastard wing (alula). Where they join the bone within the wing, the bases of the primary and secondary wing-feathers are covered by successive rows of overlying contour feathers called 'coverts'.

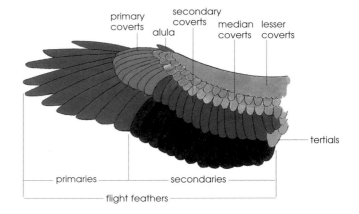

THE SIZE OF A BIRD

It is not practicable to measure a bird in standing, sitting or swimming position. This is because different species hold themselves in different ways at different times. A long-necked bird may hold its neck tucked in or outstretched; some birds are hunched, others erect. The measurements of length in this book (as in field-guides) represent the dimensions of a dead bird lying flat on a table. If its legs protrude beyond its tail, they are included in the total measurement. Where a species has seasonally long tail plumes, these have not been included in the measurement of length.

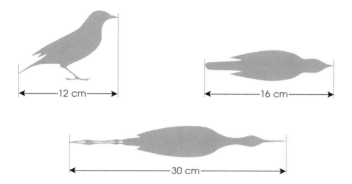

To remember the size of a bird, it is a good idea to compare it with three common birds that you know, for example a House Sparrow, Feral Pigeon and Helmeted Guineafowl. Is it larger or smaller than any or all of these species? You can use this comparison as a yardstick both when trying to visualize a bird and when you are taking notes on a bird that you have seen and wish to identify.

House Sparrow

Feral Pigeon

Helmeted Guineafowl

SIX-POINT ID CHECK

1. **RELATIVE SIZE:** Larger or smaller than a species or several species that you know?
2. **BILL SHAPE, SIZE AND COLOUR:** A guide to food preference and, thus, bird group.
3. **LENGTH AND COLOUR OF LEGS:** Short, normal or long? Are they a distinctive colour?
4. **PLUMAGE COLOUR AND MARKINGS:** What are the head colours? Is there a wing-bar? Where on the bird are there any distinctive colours and markings?
5. **HABITAT:** Where did you see the bird? – an important clue.
6. **ACTIVITY:** Walking, hopping, wading, swimming? Pecking on the ground, feeding in the air or in a tree, or probing in the mud?

THE FINAL CHECK: Is the bird in the right area? Check the distribution map in your fieldguide! Is the bird in its correct habitat? If not, are you sure you have the correct bird?

Glossary

Although an effort has been made to avoid complicated terminology in this book, it is not always possible to avoid unfamiliar and technical terms – or ordinary words with unusual meanings – when describing birds. The following may be a useful list for starter birders:

arboreal   Pertaining to trees, arboreal birds being those that feed in trees. cf 'terrestrial'.

cap   Top of a bird's head, starting from the eyebrow.

cere

carpal joint   A bird's 'wrist', a forward-projecting prominence in the folded wing.

casque   Horny cap or protuberance on the bill or head of some birds.

cere   Soft base of the bill, seen in parrots, pigeons and birds of prey.

comb   Fleshy protuberance on the bill or head of a bird, as seen in the Knob-billed (Comb) Duck.

comb

coverts   Small contour feathers. See diagram on page 14.

crest   Plumes or tuft of feathers on a bird's head.

crown   Area surrounding the head below the cap, clearly seen in the Crowned Plover.

culmen   Top ridge of the upper bill (mandible), sometimes coloured as in the Hadeda Ibis.

crest

diagnostic   Characters that distinguish a species.

endemic   Related to a region; found nowhere else.

eye-stripe   Narrow band, usually black, extending from the base of the bill backwards through the eye and beyond; serves to conceal the eye. See also 'mask'.

crown

fledgling   Bird that has left the nest but is still under parental care.

front   Part of a bird's forehead adjacent to the base of the upper mandible. See diagram on page 14.

gape   Soft corner of the mouth where upper and lower bill (mandibles) are hinged; often white, cream or yellow in nestlings and fledglings.

gular region   A bird's throat.

culmen

hood   Coloured, often black, area of a bird's head extending to below the eye, as seen in the Fiscal Shrike.

juvenile   Young bird, often used for any bird below the adult stage, including nestlings and fledglings. Same as 'immature'. 'Sub-adult' is also used for a young raptor that is close to acquiring adult plumage.

hood

lamellae   Fine hair-like structures that line the bill in some birds (e.g. flamingoes), enabling them to filter small food items.

lores   Space between upper mandible and eye, i.e. the loral region.

mandible	Upper or lower jaw (bill).
mantle	A bird's upper back, between the lower hind neck and lower back.
mask	Wide black area surrounding the eye, wider than an eyestripe. Seen in many shrikes and batises and the Masked Weaver.
migrant	A species that moves temporarily from one region to another at a set time of year.
moustachial-stripe/streak	Line of colour, often black, extending from the gape.
nape	Back of a bird's head.
nestling	Bird in the nest, still under parental care.
parasitize	To lay eggs in the nest of an unrelated species and not take part in raising the chicks.
pectoral regions	Sides of a bird's upper breast.
primaries	Major flight feathers on outer part of wing. See diagram on page 14.
raptor	Bird of prey.
rictal bristles	Bristles in the region of the gape, seen in some barbets, nightjars and flycatchers.
roost:	Place where birds spend the night or (in nocturnal species) the day.
savanna	Much-misused term. In this book savanna refers to mixed-tree communities with thickets and termite mounds and open regions with grassy ground cover.
speculum	Patch of iridescent colour on secondary upperwing feathers of certain dabbling ducks.
still-hunt	To hunt by watching from a perch and then pouncing on or pursuing prey.
streak	Vertical mark, longer than a spot, as seen on the underparts of the Cardinal Woodpecker.
terrestrial	Ground-dwelling.
understorey	Lowest strata of wooded area, close to or on the ground.
vagrant	Bird found out of its normal range, usually because of adverse weather conditions or poor navigation.
wattles	Fleshy appendages, usually highly coloured, that hang from the gape or the lores.

mask

moustachial-stripe/streak

rictal bristles

day-hunting raptor (African Fish Eagle)

streaking

wattle

♂ male ♀ female **Juv** juvenile **N-Br** non-breeding **Br** breeding

Common doves

Doves and pigeons are one family. The name 'dove' is usually given to the smaller species and 'pigeon' to the larger, but there seem to be no rules on the division (see page 20).

There are 10 species of doves in southern Africa. The three most likely to be recognized are the Laughing Dove and Cape Turtle Dove, which are found everywhere except the arid Atlantic coastline, and the Red-eyed Dove, which occurs over most of our populated eastern regions. To get to know doves, concentrate first on recognizing the Laughing Dove and on differentiating between the Cape Turtle Dove and the Red-eyed Dove. They are entirely different species although they may appear at first glance to be the same.

The plumage of the **Laughing Dove** is a subtle mixture of blue-grey, cinnamon, lilac and white, with blackish flight feathers. Its call – a background to most summer mornings – is a series of soft 'doo doo DOO doo doo' sounds. It feeds on grass seeds and some insects, and is not averse to household scraps.

▲
The **Laughing Dove** (length 25 cm) shuffles about on its deep red legs in every garden or park, even on busy city pavements.

The green spots of the **Emerald-spotted Dove** ▶ (length 20 cm) are easily recognized. The two black bars across the back and black terminal bar on the tail are clearly visible in flight.
▼

W. Tarboton

SOME LESS COMMON SOUTHERN AFRICAN DOVES

Namaqua Dove

African Mourning Dove

Tambourine Dove

Cinnamon Dove

The very common **Cape Turtle Dove** is all-over grey with a narrower black half-collar than the Red-eyed Dove. Its well-known call may be heard at any time of day or night and resembles the words 'Father, why don't you work' or 'Work harder', 'Work harder' repeated over and over.

The **Red-eyed Dove** is larger and usually calls from a tall tree, often near water, sounding like 'Father, why don't you work'. It makes a 'snare' sound when settling. It has brownish-grey upperparts and the entire breast and underbody have a pinkish tinge while its crown is very pale grey, almost white. In flight its tail shows a buffy fringe, not white as in the Cape Turtle Dove. Males are larger than females.

The **Emerald-spotted Dove**, found in woodland and bushveld, belongs to a group called 'wood doves', recognized by two black bars across the back, a black terminal bar on the tail and reddish-brown flight feathers. Its call is heard frequently in the bush on a warm day, starting off slowly, a soft cooing 'du, du, dudu du du dudu du du du du . . .' sequence, which tails off at the end.

All doves walk with a crouched, shuffling action, much of the leg obscured by their body-feathers. Doves do not hop.

N. Dennis/SIL

▲ The common **Cape Turtle Dove** is found in almost every habitat in southern Africa.

The all-grey **Cape Turtle Dove** (length 28 cm) is slightly darker above than below, with a narrow, black half-collar ◀ on its hind neck.

The **Red-eyed Dove** (length ▶ 33–36 cm) has a wider neck-band than the Cape Turtle Dove and a red eye with a fleshy red surround.

European Turtle Dove

Blue-spotted Dove

Notes

- Since most pigeons and doves feed principally on grain, they must have access daily to water. Unlike most other birds they drink by immersing the bill and sucking.
- All doves and pigeons build simple nests comprised of a small platform of twigs on which two white eggs are normally laid. Nesting may occur at any time of the year, with a peak during summer.

Pigeons

Pigeons are often confused with doves (previous page) and the two terms are even interchanged. Pigeons are generally thought to be bigger than doves, but of the five species described here only the Rameron Pigeon is larger than the largest southern African dove. This shows the arbitrary way in which the 'larger' pigeon and 'smaller' dove division is made. Doves are usually more grey than their pigeon relatives.

By far the best known and most widespread pigeon is the introduced **Feral** or **City Pigeon**. This extremely common pigeon is found in large towns and cities and in industrial regions all over the world in a variety of plumage colours.

Of the four indigenous pigeons the **Rock** or **Speckled Pigeon** is probably the most common, well known for its habit of using houses in semi-rural areas as ready-made 'rocks' on which to roost. These pigeons nest on roofs, against chimneys or in outbuildings. Although they feed, occasionally, in gardens, they prefer to fly daily to grain fields in open country. Their call is a prolonged cooing 'cook cook cook . . .' rising to a crescendo and then falling.

Although it is naturally grey, with two dark bands across paler grey secondaries, the **Feral Pigeon** (length 33 cm) has evolved a variety of plumage colours including shades and speckles of brown, black and white.

The **Rock Pigeon** (length 33 cm) has a grey head, red eye mask and legs, and yellow eyes. Its upperparts are a deep red, well speckled with white, and the underparts are grey, the breast well streaked with red.

The large **Rameron Pigeon** is partial to buds and wild fruits, especially in conifer plantations. It is normally a shy bird, but small flocks will visit fruiting trees in domestic gardens in the appropriate season. The call is a deep 'croo cru'.

The **African Green Pigeon** is another nomadic fruit-eater, which is found in low-altitude woodland regions and well-wooded riverine forests and is especially attracted by ripe wild figs. It can be seen clearly in the early morning when it perches prominently on tree-tops to catch the warming rays of the sun. Its call – an unpigeon-like, explosive, high-pitched yet melodious bubbling, descending in pitch – is almost impossible to describe adequately in words.

A fifth pigeon in the southern African region is the scarce and strictly localized **Delegorgue's** or **Bronze-naped Pigeon**.

N. Myburgh

▲
The beautiful **African Green Pigeon** (length 30 cm) is basically green with mauve shoulder-patches. It has red legs and yellow 'pants', a red base to its white bill, yellow feather-edges of varying extent and a white eye.

The **Rameron Pigeon** (length 40 cm) can be identified by its bright yellow bill, legs and eye-ring, all of which are visible in flight. It has a dark maroon-red body, speckled with white, becoming pink around the neck and grey on the head.
▼

Delegorgue's Pigeon (length 29 cm) is a secretive bird of coastal and eastern ◄ montane forests.

G. Lockwood

Notes

- The Feral Pigeons of towns and cities have descended from escaped domestic pigeons used for their extraordinary homing instinct. These in turn are descended from the North African or European Rock Pigeon, a species that has been domesticated for about 2 000 years.
- In the absence of houses, Rock Pigeons actually do roost on cliffs.

Common bulbuls

There are nine bulbul species in southern Africa. Four are uncommon or difficult to find, two are rare, and three are common within their ranges. There are three well-known species – the **Black-eyed Bulbul** of the eastern half of the region, the **Red-eyed Bulbul** of the western parts (its range overlapping slightly with that of the Black-eyed Bulbul) and the endemic **Cape Bulbul** of the western and southern Cape. One or other is to be seen in the parks and gardens of almost every town. They are regular visitors to feeding tables where fruit is provided and are often surprisingly tame. They are otherwise to be found in any well-bushed region, especially in riverine bush.

Black-eyed and Red-eyed bulbuls have cheerful chattering calls and are similar in appearance and behaviour. The Cape Bulbul makes cheerful liquid sounds like 'piet piet patata' or 'piet majol'. All three species are basically blackish brown with black or dusky tufted heads and characteristic lemon-yellow undertail coverts. Their smallish bills, adapted to a diet of fruit and insects, are black, as are their legs. The sexes are alike.

While it is similar in appearance to the Black-eyed Bulbul, the **Red-eyed Bulbul** (length 19–21 cm) has dark brown eyes surrounded by a bright orange-red orbital ring.

The **Black-eyed Bulbul** (length 20–22 cm) has a dusky brown upper breast and mantle which contrast with its black, tufted head. Its belly is a dusky white and its dark brown eyes appear black.

The dark brown eyes of the **Cape Bulbul** (length 19–21 cm) are surrounded by a conspicuous white eye-wattle, widest in front. The dark brown area on the head extends over the shoulders to mid-breast and the underbelly is whitish.

P. Steyn

Notes

- Bulbuls are among the first birds to spot a predator, be it a snake, mongoose, raptor or domestic cat. They set up a loud, on-going chattering that draws in other birds, each adding to the noise. until the predator leaves.
- The crest on a bulbul's head is erectile. It is flattened when the bird is relaxed and raised when the bird is alarmed or in company with other birds as at a bird feeder.

SOME LESS COMMON SOUTHERN AFRICAN BULBULS

| Sombre Bulbul | Yellow-bellied Bulbul | Terrestrial Bulbul | Slender Bulbul | Yellow-streaked Bulbul | Stripe-cheeked Bulbul | Bush Blackcap |

White-eyes

These tiny yellow-green birds with 'spectacles' are common all over southern Africa. They occur in most gardens, flocks of birds gleaning small insects, such as aphids, from the canopies of trees and creepers. White-eyes prefer riverine woodland and well-wooded urban areas. One or another of the three southern African species can be found in all but the most arid parts of the region. They have a closely similar call while foraging, a melancholy 'phe'. In summer they sing a loud, rambling song.

The **Cape White-eye** has three distinct colour forms. In the south and south-west of the region it has grey underparts and green upperparts, only the throat being yellow. In the north and east, its underparts are a greenish yellow (greener in KwaZulu-Natal). Inter-grading occurs where the three colour forms meet.

The **Orange River White-eye** occurs in the Orange (Gariep) River region and northwards into western Namibia. However, its behaviour patterns are similar to those of the other species. The smaller **African Yellow White-eye** is found in the more tropical regions of southern Africa and beyond, its range just tipping into South Africa in the far northern Kruger National Park. This is the common white-eye of northern Botswana, Zimbabwe and Mozambique.

The **Cape White-eye** (length 12 cm) has green upperparts and greenish-yellow underparts in its **northern** form.

The **southern form** of the Cape White-eye has a yellow throat and grey underparts.

The underparts of the **eastern form** of the Cape White-eye are even greener than those of its northern counterpart.

The **African Yellow White-eye** (length 10,5 cm) is much yellower than the other species, pure yellow below and very pale green above.

The **Orange River White-eye** (length 12 cm) has pale yellow to whitish underparts. The cinnamon wash on its flanks is sometimes obscured by its wings.

Sparrows

Sparrows are small, sturdy, seed-eating birds related to weavers. Their strong beaks are short and conical for crushing grain, and are black when the bird is breeding and yellowish or pinkish at other times. All southern African sparrows have diagnostic chestnut-brown mantles and wings, with a small, white patch on the upperwing coverts near the shoulder. The rest of their plumage is grey and white, often with some black on the head.

The **Cape Sparrow** is virtually an endemic resident and prefers urbanized regions, frequenting parks and gardens. It is also common in farmlands and may form large nomadic flocks when not breeding. Both sexes have black bills and legs when breeding. Their call is 'chirrup, chip, chop'.

The **House Sparrow** is probably the best-known sparrow, found everywhere in southern Africa except the central Kalahari. Common or abundant in Europe, it has spread to many parts of the world over the last hundred years, often with human assistance. The local race has evolved from birds introduced from Britain and India. It is entirely omnivorous and is seldom seen away from urban dwellings, living commensally with humans and relying, to a large extent, on household scraps. It will locate even small settlements. Its call is 'chee-ip' or 'chissik'.

♂

♀

In the **Cape Sparrow** (length 15 cm) the male has an all-black head, throat and upper breast dissected by a broad white 'C'. The female is similar but paler, the head grey and the 'C' less evident.

LESS COMMON SOUTHERN AFRICAN SPARROWS

Great Sparrow

Yellow-throated Sparrow

Frequently seen but less common is the **Southern Grey-headed Sparrow**. It enters well-wooded gardens and can be attracted to feeding tables with seeds. The call is a high-pitched 'cheep-chirp', the first note descending, the second ascending, and is often the first indication of its presence. Like the Yellow-throated Sparrow, the Southern Grey-headed Sparrow walks; it does not hop on the ground like most other sparrows. When breeding, Southern Grey-headed Sparrows have black bills, which are otherwise horn-coloured.

P. Steyn

The **Southern Grey-headed Sparrow** (length 15–16 cm) has an entirely mid-grey head and whitish underparts. The sexes are similar.

♂

W. Tarboton

W. Tarboton

The **House Sparrow** (length 14–15 cm) has a narrow black bib in the male, widening onto the upper breast. The male's white cheeks contrast with its pale grey underparts. The female (below) is much paler and has a pink bill and legs and no bib. Young birds are even drabber and paler than the females.

Notes

SPARROWS' NESTS
- The Cape Sparrow builds a large, untidy, ball-shaped nest of dry grasses and scraps of paper, wool and plastic, with an entrance at one end. It places the nest quite conspicuously in a tree.
- The House Sparrow's nest is similar but less bulky and is usually placed beneath the tiles of a house, in a drainpipe or under thatch.
- The Southern Grey-headed Sparrow differs from most sparrows in that it nests in a tree-hole, often one excavated by a woodpecker or barbet. Alternatively, it uses a hole in a wall, lining the nest chamber with soft plant material.

Mousebirds

The **Red-faced Mousebird** (length 34 cm) has red facial skin, pale blue eyes, a black bill and deep red feet. Its plumage is brownish except for pale grey underparts and rump.

Mousebirds probably get their name from their long tails and the way they clamber about fruit-bearing trees. The three southern African species are small-bodied and mostly brown or grey, with crested heads, hair-like plumage and long, stiff tails. All three are common species within their distributions. The White-backed are found mostly in the west and the Speckled in the east.

Mousebirds live and feed in flocks. They gather in bushes or thickets, each bird appearing to crash down without selecting a specific perch. When two or more species occur in the same area, one is generally more common. All species are highly gregarious and sedentary, no long-distance movements having been observed. Their flight behaviour normally involves a brief period of fast wing-flapping followed by a glide.

The aptly named **Red-faced Mousebird** is the most widespread, its preferred habitat being thickets in woodland and riverine bush. It subsists mainly on berries, vegetation and nectar. The birds can be identified in the air by the compact groups in which they fly, calling a descending 'tree-ree-ree'.

The widespread **Speckled Mousebird** frequents dense bush, orchards and gardens in the wetter areas. The birds gather in flocks of up to 20 individuals and can become a nuisance. Speckled Mousebirds fly in straggling procession, their call a rasping 'zwit-wit'. They have the same diet as Red-faced and White-backed mousebirds, with a distinct preference for fruit and seedlings. Speckled and White-backed mousebirds visit bird tables where fruit is offered. The Red-faced Mousebird is less inclined to do so.

W. Tarboton

The **Speckled Mousebird** (length 34 cm) is a drab brown, its breast lightly barred. It has a dark eye in a small, black facial-mask, a bill that is black above and white below and black feet.

The **White-backed Mousebird,** an endemic resident, is found in the drier parts of the region, often in thornveld where it feeds on fruit, buds and young leaves and on nectar when available. White-backed Mousebirds also fly in straggling order, one following another at intervals. Their call, while feeding, is 'zwee, wewit'.

Three other species of mousebird occur north of our borders: Blue-naped (closely related to the Red-faced), Bar-breasted (closely related to the Speckled) and White-headed mousebirds. They are very similar in behaviour and appearance and, like all mousebirds, are exclusively vegetarian.

In some parts of the world, mousebirds are called colies (coly in the singular), which stems from their generic name *Colius.*

The **White-backed Mousebird** (length 34 cm), seen on its nest (above) and in typical pose (left), has grey upperparts and tail, a white back, maroon rump and buffy underparts. Its bill is white with a black tip to the upper mandible, and it has black eyes and red feet.

Notes

- Mousebirds often hang by their feet, sometimes facing the early morning sun to warm their bodies, their heads well below the chosen branch. They usually sleep while hanging together in a close bunch for shared warmth. The loose, hair-like feathers that cover their underbodies probably provide less insulation than normal feathers.
- Speckled Mousebirds can become the gardener's worst enemy. They devour seedlings and fruit or damage them beyond use. Garden peas, for instance, can be demolished in a few hours.
- When courting, Red-faced Mousebirds indulge in perch-jumping display behaviour, two individuals of opposite sex jumping up and down on a branch prior to copulation. Mutual head-preening is common among courting mousebirds.

Thrushes

Thrushes belong to a large family of small birds that includes chats, wheatears and robin-chats. Five ground thrush and four rock thrush species are seen in southern Africa. They are good songsters and are heard from trees, mostly during summer. Many thrushes come into gardens, depending on locality, and two thrush species are found in evergreen forests.

Watch thrushes as they run or hop and forage for worms and familiarize yourself with their appearance and behaviour. The European Starling and Indian Mynas are similar to the thrushes in size (see page 34), but are quite different in behaviour, as are other starlings – an important clue to identity (as in the case of other bird groups).

A widespread ground thrush, the **Olive Thrush**, occurs in two colour forms or races, both common and with orange-yellow bill and legs. Race A is found in coastal and escarpment forests and Race B (the more sombre) is found inland, especially in highveld gardens. The birds feed on earthworms, insects and fruit and, when foraging, run with head lowered, then stop and stand with the back at an angle 45 degrees to the horizontal.

Race A of the **Olive Thrush** (length 20–22 cm) has a white throat speckled black, a white vent and orange underparts from breast to belly.

In Race B, only the underbelly is orange and both throat and vent are grey, not white. Throat-speckling is not always present.

The white underparts of the **Kurrichane Thrush** (length 22 cm) are washed with orange on the flanks and its bill and legs are orange. It has a distinct black streak on either side of its throat.

SOME LESS COMMON SOUTHERN AFRICAN THRUSHES

Spotted Thrush

Orange Thrush

Short-toed Rock Thrush

Sentinel Rock Thrush

Miombo Rock Thrush

The **Kurrichane Thrush** is also a common bird, which may replace the Olive Thrush in your garden. It is found in open woodlands and is brighter than the Olive Thrush, with a white eyebrow and a very distinct streak on each side of its throat. As in all thrushes, the underparts of juveniles are spotted.

The **Groundscraper Thrush** has distinct black spots on its white underparts. It gets its name from its habit of scraping with its feet among fallen leaves in its woodland habitat. The very localized Spotted Thrush (see 'Some less common thrushes', below) has similar underparts and white wing-bars. This bird occurs only in eastern coastal forests.

Rock thrushes (except for the Miombo Rock Thrush of Zimbabwe) live on rocky koppies or cliffs. Unlike ground thrushes, they have black beaks and black legs and the plumage of males and females differs. Male rock thrushes have a grey head (one species also has a white cap), deep orange-brown underparts and, sometimes, a grey back. Females have speckled brown upperparts, their underparts either whitish or washed orange or else orange-brown as in the males. Males have clear, repetitive songs and loud calls.

The **Cape Rock Thrush** is the most widespread rock thrush, occurring from the Western Cape in a broad band all the way to the east and north. Its call is a loud, ringing 'cheewoo-chirri', which is usually heard before the bird is seen.

▲
Black spots on white underparts and a very erect stance distinguish the **Groundscraper Thrush** (length 22 cm).

♀

◀ In the **Cape Rock Thrush** (length 21 cm), both male and female are more richly coloured than the other rock thrushes. ▼

♂

Notes

Despite similarities in general shape and size, there are important differences between thrushes and starlings:
- Starlings (except the Wattled Starling) are darker than thrushes, sometimes even blackish. No thrush has the iridescent colouring of the unique blue-green glossy starling group. The pale, even whitish, colour of the Wattled Starling is also not seen in thrushes.
- Unlike thrushes, starlings tend to have a strutting, even swaggering, walk and stand more erect, their backs angled at about 60 degrees to the horizontal.
- Another important difference between thrushes and starlings is that many starlings flock; thrushes do not.

Chats & robins

Chats and robins are a fairly large group of small, insectivorous, ground-feeding, slender-billed song-birds that resemble the larger thrushes in general shape. As with thrushes, the fledged young can be told by their spotted breasts.

Many chats have very sombre plumage and some species are confusingly alike. The name 'chat' comes from the 'chak, chak' call, like the sound of two stones being clapped together. Red-breasted southern African chats are traditionally called 'robins' instead of 'robin-chats', the more accurate name for many of our species. Other members of the family are called 'scrub-robins', 'alethes' or 'wheatears'. A family characteristic is the habit of jerking the tail upwards and, especially among the less colourful chats, flicking the wings while perched.

The **Cape Robin-chat** is a common and familiar garden bird in the southern and south-eastern parts of the region, usually heard in the early morning and evening. It has a pleasant, continuous song, each passage starting on the same note and involving a much-repeated 'Jan-Frederik', from which stems its Afrikaans name. Its diagnostic dull orange back and tail feathers are quite conspicuous when the bird is taking off in typically low flight.

W. Tarboton

The **Cape Robin-chat** (length 18 cm) has an orange upper breast, lower back and outer tail feathers, the upperparts otherwise earth-brown. It is blackish around the face, with a prominent white eyebrow and dusky white underbelly.

N. Myburgh

The **Natal Robin-chat** ▶ (length 18–20 cm) is almost entirely orange, with silvery grey upperparts.

SOME LESS COMMON SOUTHERN AFRICAN CHATS & ROBINS

Buff-streaked Chat   Starred Robin   Chorister Robin   White-browed Scrub Robin   Bearded Robin

The **Natal Robin-chat** is commonly found in the eastern littoral and, sparsely, inland to the lowveld. It is well known for its song and its extraordinary ability to mimic other birds as well as human whistles. This is normally a secretive species of forest undergrowth, but it freely enters well-wooded gardens in its range.

The dumpy little **Stonechat** is common both in Europe and southern Africa, except in low rainfall regions. Seldom seen in gardens, it is a bird of abandoned agricultural land and fallow plantations near wetlands. It also frequents roadside ditches, and is normally seen in pairs, which perch on low bushes or weeds in sight of each other. Females tend to more grey-brown upperparts than males, with a much paler orange underside, but retain the white rump. Although Stonechats have a short warbling song, their usual call is a quiet and repeated 'tsak, tsak'. The birds are easily overlooked on the ground. In flight, however, their white wing-bars and rump are conspicuous.

Heuglin's Robin is found mostly at lower altitudes. It spends most of the day in dense bush, even within gardens, but sings clearly in the early morning and evening, often perching conspicuously. A good songster, this robin is usually first detected by its 'pip pip ureee, pip pip uree . . .', each phrase starting quietly and working up to a crescendo.

W. Tarboton

The handsome male **Stonechat** (length 14 cm) has a black head and upperparts, a white half-collar and rump and an orange-red breast merging into white on its underbelly and vent.

In **Heuglin's Robin** (length 19–20 cm) the underparts, chin to vent, are paw-paw orange and the head black, dissected by a bold white eyebrow. The wings are greyish.

Notes

- All robin-chats are strictly territorial, defending their chosen home patch fiercely against the intrusion of others of their kind. During the breeding season these encounters may develop into physical contests in which the loser may be killed.
- Robin-chats are the favoured hosts of the summer-visiting Red-chested Cuckoo (Piet-my-vrou), which lays its egg in the host's nest, leaving the host to feed and raise the young cuckoo. The Cape Robin usually raises two broods, the first clutch laid before the migrant cuckoos arrive. It is the second clutch that is more likely to be parasitized.

| Karoo Robin | Kalahari Robin | Swynnerton's Robin |

Barbets

H. Chittenden

Barbets are small to medium-size, robust, fruit-eating birds with stout, toothed or serrated bills, many species with colourful or striking plumage. Their legs are comparatively short and are adapted to a mostly arboreal existence of climbing and clinging, the feet with two toes facing forwards and two backwards. The sexes look very similar. The name barbet is derived from the French for 'beard' and refers to the stiff bristles (their purpose unknown) that protrude from the base of the bird's bill.

The smaller barbets are called tinkerbirds (or tinker barbets) because their repetitive calls sound like a hammer on a blacksmith's anvil. Like woodpeckers, to which they are distantly related, barbets excavate nest holes in trees, using their tails as props while clinging. They have jarring or mechanical-sounding calls and do not generally 'sing'.

The striking, multi-coloured **Crested Barbet**, its yellow head and underbody well sprinkled with red, occurs in most of the eastern regions but is absent in the south and west. The male is slightly brighter than the female, both with a heavy pale yellow bill with a black tip, a

The **White-eared Barbet** (length 17 cm) has dark brown to blackish plumage, its underbelly white. It has a diagnostic white streak from eye to ear coverts.

W. Tarboton

The **Crested Barbet** (length 23 cm) may be seen in the garden, perched on a hanging feeding table. At its nest hole (right) it uses its tail as a prop, like all barbets.

LESS COMMON SOUTHERN AFRICAN BARBETS

Green Barbet

Whyte's Barbet

Golden-rumped Tinkerbird

Eastern Tinkerbird

small black crest and black bib The call of the Crested Barbet resembles the sound of an old wind-up alarm clock with the bell muffled, a high-pitched trilling 'trrrrrrrrr . . .' becoming 'kekekekek . . .' when the bird is agitated.

The conspicuous, small **White-eared Barbet** is common in the KwaZulu-Natal coastal regions, where small groups make their presence known by calling 'treetreetreetree . . .' loudly and in unison.

Also conspicuous, the **Black-collared Barbet** is common in gardens throughout the eastern half of the region. As in some other barbet species to the north, the frontal half of its head is bright red up to the ear coverts, throat and breast. The black collar, extending from the back of the head to the nape and around the breast, is thus the surer form of recognition. Black-collared Barbets are usually seen in family groups of four to five. Their peculiar, ringing call is a duet between two birds, commencing with a buzzing 'skerr skerr' and becoming 'too-puddely-too-puddely-too-puddely' repeated six to eight times in succession. The first bird calls 'too' while the second answers 'puddely' in such rapid sequence as to sound like a single bird calling. The entire group may accompany this performance, all the birds bowing and tail-raising at the same time.

▲
The **Acacia Pied Barbet** (length 17–18 cm) is the common woodland barbet of western parts of southern Africa, but also has a wide range in other areas. It is seen below with an appetizing mouthful at its nest in a tree.
▼

▲
The wings of the **Black-collared Barbet** (length 19–20 cm) are dull brown when folded, as is the upper tail. Flight- and tail-feathers have yellow edges and the whitish underparts are liberally washed with yellow.

Yellow-fronted Tinkerbird

Red-fronted Tinkerbird

Notes

- The barbets described here can be attracted to your garden with apples (pierced onto nails, as seen on the opposite page) and other fruit. They also like dampened bread and mealie meal porridge. By spearing the fruit, you can prevent the eager bird from knocking it to the ground while feeding. Be sure to place the fruit beyond the reach of pets.
- You can also attract barbets by wiring a metre-long nesting log, about 15 cm in diameter, to a tree. The barbets will excavate their own nest. Willow or sisal is easily worked, but hardwood lasts longer. Hang the log away from leafy branches, in shade or facing away from the sun.

Starlings

Starlings are small to medium-size, some with glossy or partially glossy plumage, several species well known in urban regions. They have strong legs and bills, the bill usually black, shortish and slightly decurved. They are both arboreal and terrestrial and feed on fruits and insects. With the exception of the glossy species, their calls are mostly unmusical squeaks and squawks. (For a comparison between starlings and thrushes see page 29.)

The **Cape Glossy Starling**, sometimes referred to simply as the **Glossy Starling**, is the most common and wide ranging of the glossy starling species. It is mostly green with a black bill and legs and its eyes are a rich cadmium-yellow (greyish in juveniles). Glossy Starlings feed on fruits, insects and nectar and have a pleasant 'trrr, treer, cheer' call. In poor light, before their iridescence is revealed, they may appear black.

▲ The bluish head and mantle of the **Cape Glossy Starling** (length 23–25 cm) become a radiant peacock blue-green in bright sunlight,

Two common urban starlings are the introduced **European Starling** (in Cape coastal regions) and the **Indian** (or **Common**) **Myna** (in KwaZulu-Natal and inland to Gauteng). Both occur only in association with human habitation and have

N-Br

◄ In the **European Starling** (length 20–22 cm) non-breeding males have buffy upperparts unlike the iridescent green and purple of their breeding plumage. ▼

Br

In flight the white patch on the wings of the **Indian Myna** (length 25 cm) is conspicuous. Its blackish head, upper breast and mantle fade to red-brown on wings and flanks. ►

SOME LESS COMMON SOUTHERN AFRICAN STARLINGS

| Pale-winged Starling | Pied Starling | Wattled Starling | Greater Blue-eared Glossy Starling | Burchell's Glossy Starling |

reached pest proportions in both distributions. They are mainly omnivorous and often nest under the eaves of houses.

The **Plum-coloured** or **Violet-backed Starling** is a fairly common summer resident of the extreme northern parts of the region. In poor light or at a distance, the male may appear black and white while the female, because of its drab, spotted plumage, may be mistaken for another species. Males have a pleasant slurred song.

The largest of the common starlings is the indigenous **Red-winged Starling**, which occurs widely in pairs or flocks and is often common in towns. Bill and legs are black in both sexes, the eyes dark brown. The common call is a drawn-out 'spreeeooo', but the bird also utters a variety of pleasant whistles. Compared with many other starlings, the Red-winged Starling has rather short legs and hops when on the ground. It nests in any convenient cavity, especially under the eaves of buildings. Its partiality for berries can make it a pest in vineyards.

N. Myburgh

N. Myburgh

▲ In the **Red-winged Starling** (length 22–28 cm) the male is blue-black except for brick-red wing-feathers, distinctive in flight. The female has red wings and a grey head, mantle and upper breast with dark streaking.

▲ The male **Plum-coloured Starling** ▶ (length 18–19 cm) has snow-white underparts. The drab female can be recognized by her pale yellow eyes, short black bill and yellow gape.

N. Myburgh

Notes

- Glossy starlings prefer to nest in a tree-hole. The sole exception is the Plum-coloured Starling which will select, if possible, a tubular steel fence post to nest in and incubate its eggs despite the very high temperatures in these poles in mid-summer.
- Blue-eared Glossy Starlings are told by dark ear-patches (actually patches of dark-blue mini-feathers) that often extend over the ear coverts. The absence of a dark ear patch in the Black-bellied Glossy Starling is more difficult to see than in the Cape Glossy Starling.

Lesser Blue-eared Glossy Starling

Sharp-tailed Glossy Starling

Black-bellied Glossy Starling

Common weavers

G. Lockwood

Weavers are among our most numerous birds. They are small, compact seed-eaters with the typically short, deep-based and sharply tapering bill of all seed-eaters. The bills of a few that have a more varied diet (e.g. the Cape Weaver) are slightly longer but still deep-based. In breeding plumage the yellow weavers (and the related Golden Bishop) are the only yellow seed-eaters. In the non-breeding season, the duller plumage of both males and females complicates weaver identification.

In the three common 'masked' weavers breeding males are best told by the extent of the black mask and by eye colour; females do not have masks. Male masked weavers make similar 'swizzling' sounds near their nests and when near females. The bird of that name, the **Masked Weaver**, is the most widespread yellow weaver. Non-breeding males and females are a dull olive-green-grey, with only a slight yellow wash on the buff breast, a whitish throat, and a pink bill.

The slightly larger **Spotted-backed Weaver** also has dark red eyes. In southern Africa the top of the male's head is entirely yellow down to its bill. North of the Limpopo River, the male is more likely to

▲
The male **Cape Weaver** (length 16–18 cm) is mostly yellow in breeding plumage, with a burnt-orange flush to the head and throat, pale yellow eyes and a sharply pointed black bill.

The female **Spotted-back Weaver** is best told by its yellow eyebrow, pure yellow throat and breast, and white belly.
▼

In the **northern form** the male ▶
Spotted-backed Weaver has an entirely black head.

In the **Spotted-backed Weaver** ▶
(length 17 cm) the male's mask extends in an elongated black point down the throat as far as its upper breast. Males change little when not breeding.

♂   ♂

♀

LESS COMMON SOUTHERN AFRICAN WEAVERS

Olive-headed Weaver

Yellow Weaver

Forest Weaver

Golden Weaver

Brown-throated Weaver

Red-headed Weaver

have a completely black head, differing from the Black-headed Oriole mainly in its smaller size and black bill (unlike the oriole's orange-red bill).

The **Cape Weaver** is another common weaver, a local endemic which occurs in a wide band from the Western Cape around the coast and north to a latitude of about 24 degrees. It is a bird of well-watered farmlands and urban regions. Females and non-breeding males are olive-brown above and whitish below, with a yellow wash over the face and breast. The eyes are dark brown in the female. The bill-shape of this weaver indicates a more insectivorous and herbivorous diet.

A common coastal weaver is the all-yellow **Spectacled Weaver**. Bill shape indicates a diet similar to that of the Cape Weaver.

The male **Thick-billed Weaver** (length 18 cm) with its massive bill and neat nest is a good example of a brown weaver.

The male **Spectacled Weaver** (length 15–16 cm) is a yellow weaver with a distinctive black bib and, in both sexes, a burnt-orange wash over the head, pale yellow eyes and a slender black mask.

Female and non-breeding male **Masked Weavers** are a dull olive-green-grey, with only a slight yellow wash on the buff breast, a whitish throat, and a pink bill.
▼

The **Lesser Masked Weaver** (length 14 cm) is told by its pale yellow eyes. The mask of the breeding male extends over the bird's central crown. In females and non-breeding males the underparts are entirely yellow and the bill pink.

In the **Masked Weaver** (length 15 cm) the breeding male's black mask extends in a narrow band across its forehead adjacent to the base of the upper bill.

Notes

- All the weavers described here prefer to build their nests over water. Weavers' nests (illustrated in *Newman's Birds of Southern Africa*) are a guide to identity. Among Lesser Masked Weavers, the new nest of the season is attached to that of the previous year and one occasionally sees a colony with as many as four nests joined.
- It is a fallacy that weavers pick leaves off branches surrounding their nests to prevent snakes from entering. Snakes can enter a weaver's nest with ease, leaves or no leaves. The true purpose of leaf-stripping is to allow the male to be seen when it is hanging under the nest flapping its wings to attract a female. Performers need an open stage!

Red-billed Buffalo Weaver

Chestnut Weaver

White-browed Sparrow-weaver

Sunbirds

Not to be confused with the hummingbirds of North and South America, sunbirds are mainly an African group with a few species in the Middle East. They are small to very small (average length 10–15 cm although the long-tailed male Malachite Sunbird reaches 25 cm), with a long, slender decurved bill and long tubular tongue that enable them to obtain nectar by probing flowers. Many species feed on small insects in the flowers, and a few search actively for spiders.

The males of most sunbird species are very colourful, with iridescent plumages. So too are some females, but the majority are drab and lack lustre. Some male sunbirds temporarily lose much of their brilliant plumage in the non-breeding period. Females of different species are often closely similar and care is necessary when identifying them, size and length of bill being important criteria. Sunbirds feed mostly on plants with tubular flowers, such as aloes, ericas and *Leonotus* species. Males at flowers usually chase away other males.

The **Malachite Sunbird** is the largest in the family, the plumage of the male an iridescent green except for the black wings and tail. This distinctive sunbird is common in Cape fynbos, where it feeds on proteas, aloes, *Watsonia* and *Leonotus* plants, and also in scrubby karoo and on mountain slopes as far north as Gauteng. There is a small population in eastern Zimbabwe. The call is a much-repeated 'chit chit chit chew chew chew . . .'

♀

♂

▲
In the male, the **Black Sunbird** (length 15 cm) has a glossy green forehead and a mauve throat, shoulder-patch and rump (visible in good light). The female has brown upperparts and off-white underparts, a dusky throat and, just below the eye, a creamy white moustachial-streak.

The male **Greater Double-collared** ▶
Sunbird (length 14 cm) showing its broad red breast-band and long bill.

N. Myburgh

SOME LESS COMMON SOUTHERN AFRICAN SUNBIRDS

Collared Sunbird   Grey Sunbird   Scarlet-chested Sunbird   Marico Sunbird   Purple-Banded Sunbird

A common and widespread sunbird of mixed bushveld, woodland and suburbia is the **White-bellied Sunbird**, a frequent visitor to gardens. Males sing from the tree-tops (a loud 'chu-ee chu-ee-chuee-trrrrr') for long periods, and both sexes hover in porches and against window recesses in search of spiders.

The common **Lesser Double-collared** and **Greater Double-collared sunbirds** are similar, males of both species having an iridescent green head, a blue band above the breast and mantle, a bright red lower breast-band, and a pale grey belly. Females are inconspicuous, dark grey-brown above and pale grey below, and are best told by bill length. The Lesser Double-collared Sunbird is a low-altitude species found in a coastal band from the Western Cape north to KwaZulu-Natal and beyond. The Greater Double-collared Sunbird is a high-altitude bird of mountain and highveld with a similar distribution.

The large **Black Sunbird** is seen singly or in pairs in broad-leaved woodland and, quite often, in suburbia. The call is either a single 'zit' or a stuttering 'chichichichchi'.

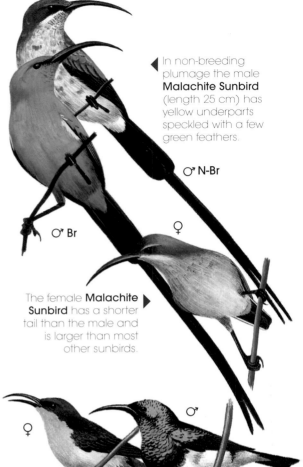

In non-breeding plumage the male **Malachite Sunbird** (length 25 cm) has yellow underparts speckled with a few green feathers.

♂ N-Br

♂ Br   ♀

The female **Malachite Sunbird** has a shorter tail than the male and is larger than most other sunbirds.

♀   ♂

Both sexes of the **White-bellied Sunbird** (length 11,5 cm) have white underparts – a good identification feature for the female. The male has a blue-green head, breast and mantle.

N. Myburgh

The male **Lesser Double-collared Sunbird** (length 12,5 cm) showing its narrow red breast-band and fairly short bill.

Notes

- Most male sunbirds have coloured 'pectoral-tufts', usually yellow, orange or red, which are concealed beneath the bird's wings at the sides of the breast (the pectoral region). These tufts are displayed at will, usually when the bird is excited.
- In general, sunbirds seem most attracted to red and orange flowers. They feed by clutching the stem of the plant and may even stand on large blossoms. They seldom feed by hovering like humming-birds. Those with short bills obtain nectar from long flowers by piercing the base or else feed on insects.

Violet-backed Sunbird   Orange-breasted Sunbird   Eastern Olive Sunbird

True shrikes

True shrikes are small, mainly insectivorous birds of open woodland. The Fiscal Shrike, Red-backed Shrike, Long-tailed Shrike and Puffback, all of which are easily seen and recognized, are grouped as true shrikes. True shrikes are told by their habit, when disturbed, of dropping off their perch and flying low before sweeping up to the next perch. They have a characteristic heavy-headed appearance with a strong, sharply hooked bill and strong feet with sharp claws. They catch prey with their feet in the manner of raptors, but are not classed as such. Three related groups of shrikes are described separately here (see pages 86–89).

The **Fiscal Shrike**, a well-known black-and-white shrike, is common in urban areas, farmlands and roadsides, often perched conspicuously on a branch, fence or telephone wire. It is called 'Jackie Hangman' for its habit of catching rodents, small birds, lizards and large insects and impaling them on a thorn or fence wire. Fiscal Shrikes in the drier western regions of southern Africa often have white eyebrows, a feature that is seldom seen in eastern shrikes.

▲ The black upperparts of the **Fiscal Shrike** (length 23 cm) are divided by a bold white wing-bar stretching to its shoulder. The female has rufous flanks.

◀ The male **Red-backed Shrike** (length 18 cm) is distinguished by a black mask, grey cap, red-brown upperparts and white underparts.

SOME LESS COMMON SOUTHERN AFRICAN SHRIKES

Lesser Grey Shrike   White-crowned Shrike   White-tailed Shrike   Brubru   Souza's Shrike

The **Red-backed Shrike** is smaller than the Fiscal Shrike but similar in shape and behaviour. It is a common non-breeding summer visitor to bushveld regions, migrating to southern Africa from Europe in enormous numbers. It is the shrike most often seen in bushveld (from October to March), prominently perched on bushes. Females are the same size, but lack the grey cap and have fine brown scalloping on their underparts.

The black **Long-tailed Shrike** has a broad white wing-bar. It occurs in bushveld and woodland, usually in small groups of three to eight birds which perch fairly low in sight of one another, often calling 'prooit-preeoo', the first phrase descending, the second ascending.

The **Puffback** is another black-and-white shrike of woodlands, but also enters well-wooded gardens with large trees. It has black upperparts, conspicuous white wing-markings and white underparts. But for its 'chik-WEEOO, chik-WEEOO' call, it is easily overlooked as it forages through tree canopies.

♀

♂

♂

The **Puffback** (length 18 cm) normally has dark red eyes, but in some regions the eyes may be yellow or orange. When excited, the male erects its white back feathers to form a puff.

A male **Puffback** at its nest. The female has a black cap, the male a black hood. ▶

The male **Long-tailed Shrike** (length 50 cm) has a longer tail than the female (length 40 cm). ▲

Notes

- The Fiscal Shrike is easily confused with the Fiscal Flycatcher but has a heavy hooked bill (unlike the latter's slender, non-hooked bill) and its white wing-bar reaches the shoulder. The name 'fiscal' relates to its resemblance to the feared Fiscal Tax Collector in the Cape Colony whose uniform was black and white. It seems that the black-and-white shrike's predatory habits made it as feared as the tax collector. The Fiscal Flycatcher, unfortunately, has similar plumage (see page 83) and is obliged to share the same epithet.

Wagtails

Wagtails are easily recognized by the almost non-stop bobbing of their long or very long tails. The up-and-down wagging (not side-to-side as the name suggests) of the tails of these friendly birds is described as 'pumping' since it usually involves the rear end of the body. A few related pipits also bob their tails on occasion, but never as frequently as wagtails. Wagtails show little fear of humans and are prepared to forage close to human activity. They are insectivorous and are normally found near water or in damp locations.

The **Cape Wagtail** is the most common and widespread southern African wagtail, absent only from the more arid central regions. In many urban areas the local sewage plant is much patronized by Cape Wagtails, usually strutting around in pairs uttering their cheerful calls. They also frequent local rivers and streams and homes with well-watered gardens. The call is a cheerful 'tseee-eep'.

▲
The **Cape Wagtail** (length 18 cm) is coloured in shades of grey. Only its chin and throat are pure white. The black breast-band is absent in some races.

A LESS COMMON (SUMMER-VISITING) WAGTAIL

Grey Wagtail

▲
The grey cap and mantle of the **Long-tailed Wagtail** (length 19–20 cm) are separated by a white eyebrow and pure white underbody with a narrow black breast-band. Wings and upper tail are black, all major feathers edged white.

In all eastern lowveld regions the Cape Wagtail is replaced by the **African Pied Wagtail**, a common garden bird in Zimbabwe, its call a 'tu-wee, twee twee twee'. It is almost identical to the Cape Wagtail in general behaviour and is particularly common in association with large dams, rivers and other open-water impoundments, and even rocky seashores. Its distribution extends westwards only in association with major rivers. Outside of the breeding season Cape and African Pied wagtails form small flocks that share secluded roosting places.

▲ The **African Pied Wagtail** (length 20 cm) is totally black and white with a broad black chest-band and entirely white underparts.

The **Long-tailed Wagtail** is localized on fast-flowing, perennial upland streams of the eastern escarpment from the Eastern Cape northwards to eastern Zimbabwe and beyond. It is tolerant both of open and forest streams but remains within the watercourse. Pairs jump and flit from rock to rock and forage even while wading in shallow, fast-moving water. The tail (extra long as the name suggests) and rear body are seldom still, bobbing up and down through all the bird's activities. It calls 'chirrup' when taking off, but otherwise sings 'ti-tuu-tui-tui-tui'.

Africa is visited in summer by the migrant **Yellow Wagtail**, a species with numerous plumage variations. A non-breeding Palearctic migrant, it may be seen in open marshy grasslands with short grass and on well-grazed and trodden fringes of dams and rivers. It may become numerous locally on flooded grasslands in the Okavango Delta in northern Botswana.

▲ Head patterns vary among **Yellow Wagtail** (length 18 cm) races, yellow and mid-grey hoods being the most common in southern Africa.

Notes

- The Cape Wagtail readily uses objects such as hanging flower pots as nest sites and even, in a notable case, a small motorboat. When the owners took boat trips at weekends the parent wagtails followed, catching insects on the wing to feed their growing chicks under the seat of the boat!
- Cape Wagtails often hover briefly over swimming pools to pluck an insect from the surface. They have also been seen standing on the hose of automatic pool cleaners to catch insects stranded against the hose.

African Hoopoe & woodhoopoes

N. Myburgh

Although hoopoes and woodhoopoes share decurved bills, an insectivorous diet and hole-nesting behaviour, they have evolved in entirely different ways.

The **African Hoopoe** is closely related to the European Hoopoe. It is a ground-feeder with cinnamon plumage and a prominent erectile crest. The complicated black-and-white patterning on its upper wing and rump is revealed in its markedly undulating flight.

The name 'hoopoe' is onomatopoeic, resembling the 'hoophoop, hoophoophoop' sound of the call, which is frequently heard in spring and early summer. The African Hoopoe's preferred habitat is mature woodland. It also frequents well-wooded suburbia, but is reluctant to visit feeding tables. Tree holes and cavities in walls are favoured nesting places.

Among the representatives of woodhoopoes in southern Africa is the common **Red-billed Woodhoopoe**, which appears mostly black in the field. A green gloss is visible at close range on its head and mantle, the source of its alternative name **Green Woodhoopoe**, most often used in East Africa, where three different species of woodhoopoes and one species of scimitarbill have red bills.

Red-billed Woodhoopoes are sociable birds and are usually seen in family groups of up to eight individuals, frequently drawing attention to themselves by their chorus of shrill cackling. They feed mostly in trees, probing beneath the bark and in cavities, and nest in tree-holes. Males are larger than females. The plumage of the less

▲ The **African Hoopoe** (length 27 cm) usually raises its large, striking, black-tipped crest after it settles or when alarmed.

N. Myburgh

Nestlings are fed insects and grubs by both the male and female **African Hoopoe** at intervals of a few minutes. ▶

common **Violet Woodhoopoe**, which is localized in Namibia, has a purple gloss but it is otherwise very similar to the Red-billed Woodhoopoe.

The **Common Scimitarbill** is a woodland bird differentiated from other woodhoopoes by its markedly decurved bill, blue-black to purple-black plumage, black legs and bill. Usually seen singly or in pairs, these birds feed quietly in trees and are easily overlooked. Their call, a soft 'qwep, qwep, qwep . . .' is not far-carrying.

The **Red-billed Woodhoopoe** (length 30–36 cm) has a bright red decurved bill and red feet (black in young birds). Its long graduated tail has white spots on the outermost feathers. ▶

The **Violet Woodhoopoe** (length 40–42 cm) is sometimes considered a race of the Red-billed Woodhoopoe.

The **Common Scimitarbill** (length 24–28 cm) is best identified by its markedly decurved black bill.

African Hoopoe

Red-billed Woodhoopoe

Common Scimitarbill

Notes

- Woodhoopoes in a group usually call collectively – a very loud cackling accompanied by exaggerated bowing while whipping their tails up and down. They forage from the base of a tree and work their way upwards before flying off to repeat the process at the next tree.
- Woodhoopoes probe the nests of other birds in search of fly grubs and other insects and in so doing may toss out small chicks or eggs. Sparrows and weavers justifiably regard them with suspicion and may chase them away.
- Fledgling African Hoopoes are tended and fed by their parents for about five days after they leave the nest. At this stage they do not have the adult call but instead call 'sweet, sweet'.

Prinias & prinia-like warblers

W. Tarboton

▲
The broad black chest-band of the **Black-chested Prinia** (length 13–15 cm) in breeding plumage is unmistakable. In winter, in non-breeding plumage (below), the chest-band is absent.
▼

A LESS COMMON SOUTHERN AFRICAN PRINIA

Saffron or Drakensberg Prinia

These little birds are recognized by a combination of body size, a long narrow tail (longer than their bodies) that is mostly held erect, and a monotonous 'chip-chip-chip . . .' call. All are brown above and pale below, with or without the spotted breast, and most have pale brown eyes and pink-brown legs.

The **Black-chested Prinia** is a dry-country bird with a mainly westerly distribution. It is entirely absent from all coastal regions except in the far north of Namibia. The call is either 'chip-chip-chip . . .' or 'zrrrrt-zrrrrt-zrrrrt . . .' The Cuckoo Finch (see page 108) parasitizes the nest of the Black-chested Prinia, which raises its chicks at the expense of its own.

The **Tawny-flanked Prinia**, a common garden bird in many towns, has a more easterly distribution and prefers higher rainfall zones. It is absent from much of the Cape Province, Lesotho and Namibia, but extends westwards through northern Botswana and the Cunene River region. It is found in family groups in tall,

▲
The **Tawny-flanked Prinia** (length 10–15 cm) has white underparts washed cinnamon-brown from flanks to vent and upper tail coverts and a distinct brown eye-stripe which contrasts sharply with the white eyebrow.

tangled grass in thornveld, thickets in woodland and in domestic gardens, where it can be located by its plaintive bleating 'sbreeeee, sbreeeee . . .'

The widespread and endemic **Karoo Prinia** extends from the Karoo to both west and east coasts and northwards to Lesotho. It occurs in karoo and fynbos scrub or grasslands and scrub at higher altitudes.

The outward appearance of the endemic **Namaqua Warbler**, once known as the Namaqua Prinia, strongly suggests a prinia, but its call and behaviour are different. It is found in tangled thorn thickets along Karoo watercourses. Another karoo warbler with a prinia-like long tail, often held erect, is the **Rufous-eared Warbler** which spends much time on the ground and prefers to run rather than fly.

N. Myburgh

▲ The rufous ear coverts (seen here in the male) of the prinia-like **Rufous-eared Warbler** (length 14–16 cm) are diagnostic. They are paler in the female.

The tail of the **Rufous-eared Warbler** is characteristically held upright.
▼

G. Lockwood

▲ A **Karoo Prinia** (length 14 cm) with its dark brown upperparts, heavily streaked breast and dark eyes.

Notes

- The territorial calls of all prinias are similar and are easily confused, especially as most will respond to the taped call of the Tawny-flanked Prinia. Best check your bird by sight and distribution.

▲ The **Namaqua Warbler** (length 14 cm) has rufous-brown upperparts, dark eyes and narrow black streaking only on its breast.

Swallows & martins

Swallows and martins are small aerial birds that catch and feed on day-flying insects. They belong to the same family, characterized by very short beaks with wide gapes and by short legs. There are 20 swallow and 6 martin species in the southern African region.

Martins tend to have short, squarish tails whereas many swallows have forked tails with long tail-streamers. Most swallows have glossy blue-black upperparts and pale underparts and build nests from mud pellets collected at puddles.

Martins are mostly brown, with or without pale underparts, and many excavate tunnels in earth.

Watching swallows with binoculars is not easy as they frequently twist and turn or change direction. Although male swallows may have longer tail-streamers than females, the sexes are very similar. Swallows are easily confused with swifts (see page 104), which are quite unrelated but have similar feeding and flight patterns. Rainfall is essential for many swallows to breed.

Juv

▲
The adult **European Swallow** (length 18 cm) is easily recognized by its blackish throat and brick-red chin against otherwise white underparts. Juvenile birds are also common from October to December.

The **Greater Striped Swallow** (length 20 cm) has white sides to its head, a smaller orange hood than the Lesser Striped Swallow and lightly streaked underparts. Its rump is pale orange. ▶

A **Lesser Striped Swallow** (length 16 cm) showing its extensive orange cap and densely streaked underparts. Its rump is a rich orange. ▶

SOME LESS COMMON SOUTHERN AFRICAN SWALLOWS & MARTINS

Red-breasted Swallow

Mosque Swallow

Blue Swallow

South African Cliff Swallow

Pearl-breasted Swallow

Grey-rumped Swallow

In southern Africa the most numerous swallow by far is the **European Swallow** which, in the southern spring, migrates in millions to Africa from its northern breeding grounds, returning home to breed at the end of our summer. Among resident swallows, the most likely to be seen around homes are the **Greater Striped Swallow** and **Lesser Striped Swallow**, both of which tend to make their mud nests under the eaves of houses.

The **House Martin** is probably the most common, non-breeding migrant martin to visit southern Africa in summer. It is white below and (unlike other martins) has swallow-like glossy blue-black upperparts. Although numerous, it is not easily seen since flocks tend to fly at a great height during the day when feeding and descend to lower altitudes only towards evening. The **Banded Martin** is resident in many parts of southern Africa and a summer breeding visitor in others. Flocks forage over grasslands near water, their flight slow and leisurely. They excavate nest burrows in river banks and termite mounds.

Watch near rivers and in wetlands for the **White-throated Swallow** with its single narrow breast-band. It is seldom seen far from water, where it hunts flying insects on the surface, and often nests under culverts and small bridges, even on nearby houses or outhouses.

▲ The **White-throated Swallow** (length 17 cm) is told by its clear white underparts and black breast-band.

▲ A **White-throated Swallow** feeding its nestlings.

P. Steyn

▲ The **Banded Martin** (length 17 cm) has brown upperparts and breast-band and white underparts. It has a small white eyebrow and short legs, and its square-cut tail is visible in flight.

Notes

- A swallow's bill is an insect-net. While feeding in flight it keeps its mouth wide open, catching a variety of small flying insects, often called 'aerial plankton'. Swallows usually fly in a leisurely manner, the larger species making frequent glides (something not often seen in rapid-flying swifts).
- Like many other migrant bird species, European Swallows are caught and ringed every year. The record flight for a European Swallow from South Africa to Britain is 28 days.

| Black Saw-wing Swallow | Sand Martin | Brown-throated Martin | Rock Martin |

Crows

Typically, crows are large, black or mostly black, heavy-billed, strong-legged, omnivorous birds with harsh calls. The sexes are alike. The success of the family as opportunistic scavengers probably stems from the ability to exploit a wide range of food items, from jetsam at the seashore to carrion or vegetable matter. Like raptors, crows can grasp food in their feet while feeding.

The striking white-breasted **Pied Crow** is well known and widespread throughout much of southern Africa. Its call is a loud 'kwaak', often heard while the bird is in flight. In many regions this scavenger enters towns and villages, frequenting school playing fields, agricultural lands and refuse dumps in search of food. It ranges widely in pairs or small groups, and is most in evidence near informal settlements. It nests on telephone poles and pylons as well as in coniferous trees.

▲
The **Pied Crow** (length 46–52 cm) has a heavy bill and a white collar and breast that contrasts with its otherwise entirely blue-black plumage.

▲
A basketful of mischief – four young **Pied Crows** ready to fly the nest.

◄ The **House Crow** (length 43 cm), a black bird with a grey cape and breast, is an introduced species that is rapidly extending its range in coastal areas.

The **Black Crow**, also known as the **Cape Crow** or **Cape Rook**, is widespread in southern Africa. Its call – a high-pitched 'kraaa' – is well known in the region. It prefers open areas and is able to tolerate dry, even arid, cattle areas in Botswana. It is particularly drawn to croplands. Black Crows feed in pairs or in groups. They are not attracted to human settlements.

The large **White-necked Raven** is a bird of hilly regions, most likely to be seen in the eastern mountains. It is less common and more localized than the other crows. Its call is a falsetto 'kraaaak'.

A very common bird in coastal towns, particularly in Durban, Maputo and (now) Cape Town, is the small alien **House Crow**. This crow has made its way, probably ship-assisted, from the Far East to several ports on the African east coast in recent years. It is particularly commensal with human habitations, which it colonizes quickly. It is gregarious, with a shrill 'kwaa kwaa' call.

The **White-necked Raven** (length 54 cm) is told by its large size, a particularly heavy bill, black plumage and a diagnostic white half-collar.

N. Dennis/SIL

The **Black Crow** is a bird of open country and, unlike the House Crow, is not attracted to human living.

The **Black Crow** (length 48–53 cm) is entirely blue-black. Its narrow bill appears slightly longer than that of the Pied Crow.

Notes

- Pied and Black crows have probably increased their breeding ranges and those of certain raptors by nesting on telephone poles and pylons. Lanner Falcons as well as Greater Kestrels make use of crows' nests in drier regions in the absence of trees.
- It is well known that crows and mynas can be taught to mimic human speech. The birds are probably dispersed by seamen who buy them as amusing pets in the East and – after a week or two of listening to their shrieks and squawks – release them at the next port of call, where the crows soon find mates and a good living.

Cormorants
& African Darter

▲
Cape Cormorants (length 64 cm) have a yellow gular-patch at the base of the bill. They nest (above) on offshore islands, but may be observed in assemblies (below) on rocks at the coast.
▼

A **White-breasted Cormorant** (length 90 cm) at its nest,showing its green eye, white neck and greenish gular-patch. These birds perch and often nest in tall dead trees in water. ▶

THE OTHER TWO SOUTHERN AFRICAN CORMORANTS

Bank Cormorant

Crowned Cormorant

Cormorants and darters are sea or freshwater birds that catch the fish they feed on by chasing them under water. Cormorants are bulky-bodied, with stout 'S'-shaped necks and webbed feet set well back on the body. Marine cormorants have black plumages (brown when young) whereas inland species tend to be dark brown and white. After swimming, cormorants and darters stand with their wings spread, a diagnostic feature of these birds. Southern Africa has five cormorant species and a single darter, all with similar lifestyles.

Like Bank and Crowned cormorants, the **Cape Cormorant** is a marine cormorant. Black with a greenish sheen to its plumage it is common off the south-west Cape coast. Flocks are occasionally seen flying seawards in a long line, low over the water, the line sometimes rising and then falling.

The large **White-breasted Cormorant** is seen both at the coast and at inland waters, but prefers deep inland dams. Adults are told by the sparkling white lower neck and breast. Their eyes are green, bill pale greyish, and upper head, neck and underbelly black, sometimes with a white thigh-patch. Wings and upper tail are brown, with black edges to the feathers. Immature birds have entirely white underparts and are often confused with young Reed Cormorants.

The small **Reed Cormorant** or **Long-tailed Cormorant** is a freshwater bird which is very common at inland waters. It may be seen in reeds or perched on fallen tree branches drying its outstretched wings. The underparts in young birds are entirely off-white (not white as in immature White-breasted Cormorants).

The two freshwater cormorants and the **African Darter** are seen at most large dams, the settlement pans of sewage plants and bird sanctuaries with lakes where dead trees provide perches. The African Darter has a smaller body than a cormorant and a long, slender neck and head with a sharp, dagger-like bill. It swims with its body submerged and only its long neck and head above water, giving it the appearance of a snake (hence the name 'snake bird'). It spears its prey under water and then surfaces, tossing and catching its prey headfirst before swallowing it.

▲
A long, white stripe separates the chestnut-brown fore-neck of the male **African Darter** (length 79 cm) from the black hind-neck in breeding plumage. Silvery plumes extend over its upperbody, and its upper wing-coverts are edged silvery white.

An immature **Reed Cormorant** just before changing to its all-black adult plumage. ▶

▲
The **Reed Cormorant** (length 60 cm) has a black body with a small crest on its forehead, a yellow bill and red eyes. It may be seen perched at the waterside (below) with wings outstretched.
▼

Notes

- The feathers of cormorants and darters become waterlogged when they dive, making them less buoyant than other waterbirds and therefore able to stay submerged longer. The birds swim at the surface with their bodies partially submerged; under water they propel themselves with their feet, using their wings and stiff tail to steer. They make use of their hooked bills to seize fish, which they consume at the surface.

Herons, egrets & bitterns

▲ Juveniles do not have the black eyebrow.

Herons are long-legged wading birds that feed mostly in fresh water and are found at the edges of ponds, dams, pans, lakes and rivers. They range in size from the Goliath Heron (length 140 cm) to the Dwarf Bittern (length 25 cm).

Some herons are called egrets, many of them (for example, the Cattle Egret) completely white. Bitterns are a kind of smallish heron with grey or brownish streaked plumage. They are secretive and usually difficult to find. Many herons have long, hair-like feathers ('plumes') on the head, neck and back when they are breeding. They do not call, but often make a harsh 'kraak' sound on take-off.

Herons are divided into day-feeders and night-feeders. Day-feeders can be told by their slender bodies and long necks and legs. Some of the larger day-feeding herons are grey; smaller day-feeders may be buffy, dark-grey or even black. The large **Grey Heron**, a common day-feeding waterside bird, has a black stripe above the eye and two long black plumes at the back of its head. It may also have plumes on its lower neck and back.

Night herons, such as the **Black-crowned Night Heron**, have stockier bodies, short necks and shortish legs. They usually sleep by day, but are sometimes seen in the late afternoon. Night herons often eat crabs.

▲ You can identify a **Grey Heron** in flight by its plain grey underwings.

◀ The **Black-crowned Night Heron** (length 56 cm) is some-times seen flying along rivers in the evenings on its way to its nocturnal hunting grounds.

▲ The **Grey Heron** (length 100 cm) has a pale grey body and long white neck and head. Its bill and legs are yellow at all ages.

G. Lockwood

SOME LESS COMMON SOUTHERN AFRICAN HERONS, EGRETS & BITTERNS

| Dwarf Bittern | Rufous-Bellied Heron | Slaty Egret | White-Backed Night Heron | Great Bittern | Goliath Heron | Intermediate Egret |

Herons mostly fish alone, walking in the water in search of fishes and frogs. They stand very still waiting for a fish to swim close by, then quickly catch the fish with a rapid thrust of the long bill, swallowing it head first.

The **Cattle Egret** and the large **Black-headed Heron** are two common herons that do not hunt in water. These herons eat insects, mostly grass-hoppers. Cattle Egrets, often in flocks, feed alongside grazing cows or buf-faloes. They walk close to the animal's head and rush forward to catch grass-hoppers that are flushed.

Cattle Egrets (length 54 cm) breed in colonies near water, either in trees or reedbeds. At this time, in early summer, they have rust-coloured plumes on the head, back and breast and a reddish bill and legs. These nuptial plumes and colours fade after a few weeks.

The **Black Egret** (length 66 cm) is all-dark except for its yellow feet.

The **Black-headed Heron** (length 97 cm) has grey legs and bill and is normally seen away from water, feeding in grasslands. Young birds are grey (not black) on the top of the head and the neck.

You can identify a **Black-Headed Heron** in flight by its black-and-grey underwings.

Black Egrets have the unique habit of forming a canopy with their wings when fishing.

W. Tarboton

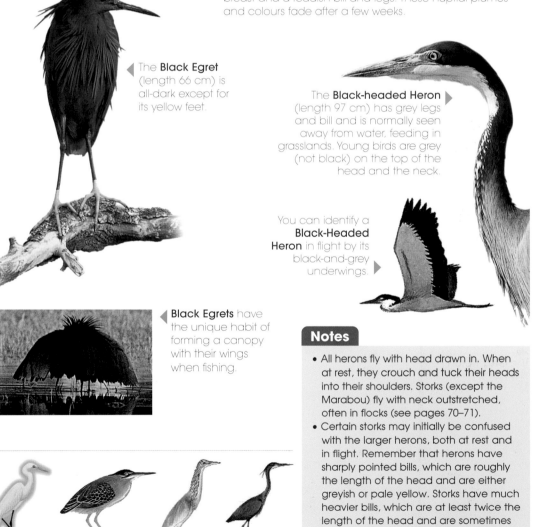

Great White Egret   Green-backed Heron   Squacco Heron   Purple Heron

Notes

- All herons fly with head drawn in. When at rest, they crouch and tuck their heads into their shoulders. Storks (except the Marabou) fly with neck outstretched, often in flocks (see pages 70–71).
- Certain storks may initially be confused with the larger herons, both at rest and in flight. Remember that herons have sharply pointed bills, which are roughly the length of the head and are either greyish or pale yellow. Storks have much heavier bills, which are at least twice the length of the head and are sometimes bright red. Several stork species also have red legs.

Ducks & geese

Ducks, geese and swans are collectively called 'wildfowl'. Swans do not occur naturally in southern Africa. A few species have been introduced, however, and can be seen in parks and private collections. Many smaller ducks are called 'teals' or (in some parts of the world) 'wigeons' or 'pochards'. Other ducks are given a single name, for example, 'garganey' or 'pintail'. In contrast with the many very colourful ducks of the northern hemisphere, African ducks tend to be rather drab. The plumage of males and females differs in some species.

There are three important types of duck. *Dabbling ducks* are the most common, usually seen swimming and 'upending', i.e. trying to reach submerged vegetation with the head and half the body underwater and the rear end sticking out of the water. Dabbling ducks 'quack' or make similar sounds. Their short legs, placed in the middle of the body, give them a horizontal stance and, being set wide apart, cause them to waddle when they walk.

The **Yellow-billed Duck** (length 53–58 cm) is a common dabbling duck which often feeds by up-ending.

P. Steyn

Like many other ducks, the **Red-billed Teal** (length 48 cm) is best recognized by its bill colour.

Pygmy Geese (length 33 cm) feed largely on waterlily seeds and are mostly found on waters where these lilies are prolific.

W. Tarboton

The mature male **Spur-winged Goose** (length 102 cm) has a fleshy swelling on its forehead.

SOME LESS COMMON SOUTHERN AFRICAN DUCKS

White-backed Duck   South African Shelduck   Hottentot Teal   Maccoa Duck   Cape Teal

Diving ducks are similar in appearance to dabbling ducks but feed by diving either to reach underwater vegetation or to catch water insects. The Southern Pochard and Maccoa Duck are typical examples of diving ducks.

Whistling ducks are so called because they really do whistle. Their legs are longer and closer together than those of dabbling ducks and are placed well back on the body, giving them an upright stance and enabling them to walk without waddling. White-faced and Fulvous ducks are typical whistling ducks.

Most ducks feed at night, spending the daylight hours 'loafing' on shorelines where they preen or rest. The best places to find them in large numbers are lakes, lagoons, pans and dams. The settlement pans at sewage disposal plants are excellent sites as are bird sanctuaries, and many municipal parks have good duck ponds. A few species visit rivers, but most prefer wider waters. Southern African ducks do not catch fish and are not normally seen at sea.

The smallest of the three southern African geese is the **Pygmy Goose**, a true goose in every sense, with a short wide-based bill and short thickish neck. Pygmy Geese are very small and are quite colourful. In contrast the brownish **Egyptian Goose** and blackish **Spur-winged Goose** are larger than most ducks, with longer bills, long necks and long legs. The Egyptian goose is especially noisy. The female calls a loud 'hur, hur, hur . . .' and the male makes a wheezy sound. Geese graze mostly on grass.

The rather drab **Cape Shoveller** (length 53 cm) is best told by its very spatulate bill, orange legs and, in flight, its pale blue upperwing panels.

White-faced Ducks (length 48 cm) are locally nomadic and travel in flocks.

◄ The **Fulvous Duck** (length 46 cm) is often seen in company with White-faced Ducks. It is the less vocal of the two species.

The male **Southern Pochard** (length 51 cm) is a handsome diving duck, darker and with a longer neck and more elegant proportions than the male Maccoa Duck, for which it is often mistaken.

Notes

- Some ducks have a 'speculum', a rectangular patch of (usually) iridescent dark-blue or green, often bordered by white on their secondary wing feathers. It is found in both sexes but is brightest in males. Birds other than dabbling ducks do not have a speculum, the true function of which is not fully understood.

African Black Duck

Knob-billed Duck

Stilt, Avocet & jacanas

G. Lockwood

These four conspicuous, long-legged species are all found at shallow inland waters. They are quite distinct and all are unmistakable.

The **Black-winged Stilt**, a white bird with contrasting black wings, is often seen in the company of Avocets, the two species being similar in feeding and other habits. The immature bird differs only in that it has a dusky patch on the head and rear neck.

Black-winged Stilts usually feed in small groups, wading and sweeping their bills over the surface of the water or probing with a rapid action, their feet lifted high with each step as they forage for small water creatures. They fly with rapid wing-beats and long legs trailing, often calling a loud 'kik-kik-kik . . .' The related black-and-white **Avocet** (or **Pied Avocet**) has long, pale grey legs and a unique slender, up-turned bill which it sweeps from side to side at the surface of the water while wading or, occasionally, swimming. Its call is a liquid-sounding 'kluut', several birds sometimes calling together.

▲ The striking **Black-winged Stilt** (length 38 cm) has very long, spindly red legs and a stiletto-like black bill. Like the Avocet, it collects insects, crustaceans, molluscs and worms from the water and muddy bottom.

Like the Stilt, the **Avocet** (length 43 cm) ▶ frequents open water, well away from bushes or surface vegetation. It keeps to the shallows, away from other large waterbirds.

The **African Jacana** is an equally distinctive waterbird with long legs and extremely long toes that spread its weight and enable it to walk on floating vegetation. Chestnut-brown wings and body, black-and-white head and neck and pale bluish frontal shield combine to make a highly diagnostic species, supported by an equally distinctive 'kyowrrr' call. The sexes are alike but the female is more heavy bodied. The bird is found at low altitudes on quiet, lily-covered pans or river backwaters where lilies flourish, seldom at highveld waters. It forages for insects beneath lily leaves and feeds on the bulbs. Where several jacanas share a pool, they indulge in frequent noisy chases over the water.

The diminutive **Lesser Jacana** is not a common species. Its stronghold in the southern African region is the Okavango Delta in northern Botswana, a habitat shared with its more colourful cousin, the African Jacana. It is often difficult to locate and, because of its very small size, is easily overlooked.

Long legs and toes present a bit of a problem for the nesting **African Jacana**, the male seen here incubating the eggs.

Juv

Both sexes of the **African Jacana** (length 40 cm) have a black stripe through the eye and a black crown. Juveniles lack the blue frontal shield.

The eye-stripe of the **Lesser Jacana** (length 16 cm) is chestnut unlike that of the juvenile African Jacana with which it might be confused.

The male **Lesser Jacana** at its nest with three beautifully marked but disproportionately large eggs.

Notes

- The females of both jacana species lay their eggs either on a lily leaf or a small pad of floating reed stems. The male bird assumes full responsibility for the incubation of the eggs and the care and raising of the young. He may be seen with the small chicks tucked under his wings, their legs hanging out.
- Female jacanas mate with several males in season, depositing a clutch of eggs after each mating. The chicks are fully mobile soon after they hatch and are able to forage for themselves, encouraged by the male who brings food items to their attention.

Flamingoes & Hamerkop

The Greater Flamingo, Lesser Flamingo and Hamerkop are three easily recognized species.

Flamingoes are long-legged, sinuous-necked, filter-feeding, wading birds with white or pinkish plumage. Worldwide, there are five highly social species, of which two – **Greater Flamingo** and **Lesser Flamingo** – occur in Africa. Both fly with neck and legs outstretched, revealing much red in their wings in contrast to the black flight feathers. Feeding flocks make a goose-like honking.

The Greater Flamingo feeds at a deep level, either wading or swimming. Its filtering devices retain food such as algae, brine shrimps and molluscs before water is expelled from the mouth. The Lesser Flamingo feeds with its bill just below the water's surface and extracts planktonic blue-green algae and diatoms.

The **Hamerkop** is a plain brown, heavy-bodied African waterbird with a backward-projecting crest. It is well known for the huge dome-shaped nest that it builds in waterside trees or overhanging rocks from sticks, grass and mud gathered on the shoreline of rivers and ponds. Barn Owls or Egyptian Geese often usurp the nest before the rightful owner can use it.

The **Greater Flamingo** (length 140 cm) is mostly white with red only on its wings. It has yellow eyes, pink legs and a pink, black-tipped bill.

G. Lockwood

The **Lesser Flamingo** (length 102 cm) is entirely pink with some red feathers on the folded wings. Its red bill appears very dark from a distance and the black tip is difficult to see.

The Hamerkop feeds on frogs, tadpoles and small fish, which it usually catches in shallow waters or below fast-running weirs. On the large African lakes, it flies to deep water and hovers briefly before diving from about five metres above the water to snatch surface-swimming fish. Usually a silent bird, it sometimes utters a nasal 'wek . . . wek . . .' which may develop into a drawn-out, high-pitched 'wek-wek-warrrrrrk'. It is not related to the storks.

Greater and **Lesser flamingoes** may feed together in groups (as seen above) in shallow soda lakes and brine lagoons. Flocks may number in the thousands,

The **Hamerkop** (length 56 cm) has a bulky-looking body and short black legs, its crest and moderately long black bill giving rise to a hammer-head appearance.

The Hamerkop's nest may measure up to a metre in diameter and take weeks to complete. The mud-lined entrance tunnel on the lower side leads to an internal nest chamber.

Notes

- Flamingoes' bills are often described as upside-down since the lower jaw is large and deep while the upper is small and lid-like. When feeding, the bird holds its bill inverted in the water and uses its tongue like a piston to pump water and mud through fine filtering lamellae surrounding the interior of the mouth.
- Evidence suggests that when flamingoes are present in large numbers in Namibia or Botswana their numbers are low in East Africa and vice versa, indicating an opportunistic movement between East Africa and southern Africa that is, possibly, brought about by weather patterns.

Ibises & African Spoonbill

Juv

The **Sacred Ibis** (length 89 cm) is white with a black head, neck and bill and some fluffy black feathers on its lower back.

Ibises are large, long-legged freshwater and terrestrial birds with long, down-curved bills. They are distantly related to storks. All ibises forage in small flocks and, like storks, fly with the neck extended. The sexes are alike. Because of the endemic Bald Ibis's restricted range and small numbers, its status is listed as Vulnerable in the Red Data Book of endangered species.

Ibises that feed in shallow inland waters or shoreline mud use the sensitive tips of their bills to probe for aquatic insects and their larvae, small fish and frogs. Those that feed away from water probe for insects such as grasshoppers, crickets, beetles and their larvae, and can seize small reptiles on the surface. Three of the four southern African ibises make little or no sound. The fourth, the Hadeda, is probably the noisiest bird in the region.

The **Hadeda Ibis** is common in many areas, its raucous voice almost deafening when uttered by a flock. Hadedas favour damp ground, including damp patches in urban gardens. Despite their noisiness, they are an asset in the garden as they probe the soil for many kinds of insects, among them red crickets and cutworms.

G. Lockwood

The rare **Bald Ibis** (length 79 cm) is named for its bald crimson head and crimson bill and legs.

The **Hadeda Ibis** (length 76 cm) has rather drab brown plumage, relieved by a pink shoulder-patch with a metallic sheen. It has a whitish cheek-line and a red top to the bill.

The **Sacred Ibis**, so-called because it was revered in ancient Egypt, is also fairly common and widespread. Its dark reddish and black legs are longer than those of the Hadeda and its black bill is longer and more curved. Flocks of Sacred Ibises are usually found close to inland waters, in marshy grounds or on rubbish tips. Another ibis of marshes is the small **Glossy Ibis**. It has a bronzy-brown head and body and blackish wings with a distinct green metallic gloss. It appears very slender in flight.

By far the most glossy and colourful of the ibises is the rare **Bald Ibis**. It lives in small flocks on rocky cliffs and feeds in grasslands, often near settlements and in very dry, hard land that has been well trodden by grazing stock. It is found in a narrow eastern strip from Lesotho northwards.

The large, white **African Spoonbill** is a distant relative of the storks. It feeds in small flocks in pans, dams, flood plains and rivers, and has an unusual feeding action, immersing its slightly open bill in the water and sweeping it sideways while wading. When it feels something edible it snaps its bill shut and in this way catches many small aquatic creatures. Spoonbills fly with head and neck outstretched. The sexes are alike.

▲ The **African Spoonbill** (length 91 cm) has long red legs, a red face and red, spoon-shaped bill. It is seen here on its nest (above) with two small chicks and in typical feeding attitude (below).
▼

▲ The metallic sheen of the **Glossy Ibis** (length 71 cm), seen here on its nest, can appear quite black at a distance. Its rust-coloured shoulder-patch is visible in good light.

Notes

- Although basically an insectivorous bird, the Sacred Ibis has the unattractive habit of foraging on rubbish dumps for insects and small rodents. Flocks also frequent colonies of nesting seabirds where they feed on discarded food items and prey on unattended hatchlings.
- Most ibis species tend to feed a long distance away from their roosts. Sacred and Glossy ibises may fly many kilometres each morning, often in spectacular 'V' formation, to reach their favourite feeding grounds.

Kingfishers

▲ The **Giant Kingfisher** (length 43–46 cm) is chestnut-breasted in the male and chestnut-bellied in the female.

♂

♀

Kingfishers range in southern Africa from small (length 13 cm) to moderately large (length 46 cm), with compact bodies, large head, short neck, tail and legs, and a powerful bill. All have striking plumage colours or patterns and a few have loud, distinctive calls.

Of the 10 kingfishers in the region, only five regularly catch fish. The other five (often found far from water) mostly seize insects and small ground creatures, which they search for from a tree perch. When a kingfisher catches a fish it carries it in its bill to a perch and thrashes it against the perch until it is stilled before swallowing it head first.

The largest kingfisher in Africa is the black-and-white speckled **Giant Kingfisher**. As its massive bill indicates, it is able to handle quite large fish. Giant Kingfishers normally frequent big rivers and their tributaries, and their loud 'kek kek kek . . .' call is often heard before the bird is sighted.

Although it is smaller than the Giant Kingfisher, the **Pied Kingfisher** is a large bird. It is usually seen at large rivers and lakes and at the seashore, the only kingfisher that regularly forages by hovering before diving. Pied Kingfishers generally occur in pairs or small family groups.

The juvenile ▶ **Malachite Kingfisher** has duller plumage than the adult and its bill is black.

The upperparts of the **Malachite Kingfisher** ▶ (length 14 cm) are a brilliant blue, even brighter on the black-speckled crown. The underparts are orange-buff, the bill and legs bright red. It also has white 'ear' patches and a white throat.

SOME LESS COMMON SOUTHERN AFRICAN KINGFISHERS

Grey-headed Kingfisher   Mangrove Kingfisher   Striped Kingfisher   African Pygmy Kingfisher   Half-collared Kingfisher

A true fisher, even on small water-bodies, is the little bejewelled **Malachite Kingfisher.** Because of its size, it is often overlooked as it perches on some slender stem over a stream before speeding off low across the water with a shrill 'peep-peep'.

Between October and March, the bushveld usually rings with the strident, descending 'yimp-trrrrrrrrrrrrrrrr' call of the **Woodland Kingfisher**, an intra-Africa migrant that visits our region to breed. This is a true woodland bird, often found in mature riverine woodland where it nests in a tree-hole. Pairs face each other with open wings when greeting.

Another woodland inhabitant is the **Brown-hooded Kingfisher,** which is common throughout the year and often seen in gardens. This kingfisher perches on a low branch from where it still-hunts for insects and other small creatures. Its loud, descending 'KIK-KIK-KIK-kik' call often betrays its presence well before it is seen.

In the **Pied Kingfisher** (length 29 cm) the female can be identified by its broad, broken, black breast-band. The male has two breast-bands, one broad and the other narrow.

The electric-blue and white **Woodland Kingfisher** (length 23–24 cm) is told by its black and red bill and strident call. It has a small black mask.

Less striking than other kingfishers, the **Brown-hooded Kingfisher** (length 23–24 cm) has a dull red bill and legs, brown-streaked head, neck and breast and a black mantle. In flight, it reveals its blue flight-feathers and tail.

Notes

- Kingfishers nest in holes, either self-excavated in riverbanks or, particularly in the case of insectivorous species, ready-made holes in trees.
- Some insectivorous kingfishers will occasionally dive into water to catch a fish. They also splash-dive to bathe.

Plovers

Plovers are stout-bodied birds with thick necks and spindly legs on which they are able to run rapidly. They have a stout bill, less long than the head, and a fairly short tail. They are strong fliers, some species migratory, and all are insect-ivorous. Plovers with head-crests, wattles or wing-spurs are sometimes called 'lapwings'. The name 'plover' is pronounced like 'clover' or 'Dover' or, more commonly, 'pluvver'.

Plovers fall into two distinct groups: the medium-sized plovers (length 24–30 cm) with erect stance and rounded wings and the small plovers (length 18–22 cm) with horizontal stance and longish wings. Eleven of the larger plovers and seven of the smaller ones are found in south-ern Africa either as residents or visitors.

One of the most prolific and confiding of the large plovers is the **Crowned Plover**, a bird of dry terrain, short or burnt grass, airfields and open ground such as car parks and grassed road fringes. Its call is a high-pitched 'kie-weeet' and, at times, a continuous noisy 'kree-kree-kree-kreeip-kreeip' while flying.

The **Crowned Plover** (length 30 cm) has a white circle around its black cap, light brown upper-parts and breast, and a white belly. It is seen below calling loudly with outstretched wings to drive an intruder from its nest.

The **Three-Banded Plover** (length 18 cm) has two black bands around the upper breast with a white band between.

SOME LESS COMMON SOUTHERN AFRICAN PLOVERS

Long-toed Plover   White-crowned Plover   Black-winged Plover   Lesser Black-winged Plover   Grey Plover

Another very common large species is the **Blacksmith Plover** with its black, white and grey plumage. It prefers wetlands, marshes, and the fringes of ponds, dams and rivers. Its name is derived from its 'klink klink klink . . .' call, like the sound of a hammer on an anvil. The **Wattled Plover**, so named for the long fleshy wattles that hang from the base of its bill, is a common wetland bird. It favours grassy waterside localities, even appearing at well-watered lawns in towns. Its call is 'kwep kwep kwep', uttered faster when the bird is agitated.

The small brown-and-white **Three-banded Plover** is common at inland freshwaters, pairs and single birds feeding in the shallows. The call is a soft 'tiuu-it'.

The large plovers may be confused with (mostly smaller) coursers (length 20–25 cm), which have a similar body shape and posture but are much less demonstrative than plovers. Coursers (see page 127) have cryptically coloured plumage, with white legs common to all but one species, and blend well with their dry habitat.

▲
The **Wattled Plover** (length 35 cm) is mostly grey-brown with black streaks on the neck, a white forehead, and a yellow black-tipped bill, yellow wattles and long yellow legs.

◀ A very common waterside resident, the striking black-and-white **Blacksmith Plover** (length 30 cm) has grey wings and mantle.

Kittlitz's Plover   Ringed Plover   Chestnut-banded Plover

Notes

- All plovers nest in a shallow scrape on the ground. If disturbed when they have eggs or chicks, the larger plovers will advance with outstretched wings or scream loudly and dive-bomb the intruder.
- Crowned, Blacksmith and Wattled plovers often perform aerial patrols of their territories in the morning during the summer breeding season. They fly around in small groups at a height of several hundred metres while calling. Their calls are similar, as are their underwing patterns.

Rails, crakes & grebes

Rails are a large and diverse family of mostly water-associated birds many of which prefer to walk rather than to swim. Frontal shields (hard, featherless, often colourful, patches that extend from the base of the bill to the top of the head) are seen in some species and may help in recognizing them. The family includes pygmy crakes, otherwise known as flufftails, which average 14–15 cm in length and are highly secretive terrestrial birds of marshes and forests, more often heard than seen. The more common and easily seen rails are described here.

The most numerous bird of the family to be seen swimming on inland waters is the **Red-knobbed Coot**. It is similar in size to many ducks, but is entirely black except for a white beak and white frontal shield, sometimes seen chasing another bird with much splashing or just standing on its floating nest. Its call is a 'cronk'.

Another frequently seen waterbird is the **Common Moorhen**, which often leaves the water and walks about displaying its yellow legs. It constantly flicks its tail upwards to reveal the white feathers beneath, and has a high-pitched 'kr-rrrrk' call.

The **Red-knobbed Coot** (length 43 cm) has two red, cherry-like balls, the same colour as its eyes, on the top of its frontal shield.

G. Lockwood

A patient wait may be rewarded by a brief glimpse of the **African Rail** (length 36 cm) with its long red bill and banded flanks.

The **Common Moorhen** (length 30–36 cm) is basically black, but has distinctive white feathers on its flanks and a bright red frontal-shield.

SOME LESS COMMON SOUTHERN AFRICAN RAILS AND GREBES

Lesser Gallinule   Lesser Moorhen   Baillon's Crake   Corncrake   African Crake

G. Lockwood

▲ The **Purple Gallinule** (length 46 cm) is usually seen alone near reedbeds.

G. Lockwood

▲ The yellow-billed, red-legged **Black Crake** (length 20–23 cm) wanders on its own in waterside vegetation.

While watching waterbirds you may see a bright bluish-green bird with red frontal-shield and beak and pink legs. It does swim, but more often walks about at the edge of the water or pops in and out of the reeds. This is the **Purple Gallinule**. Like the Common Moorhen, it flicks its tail upwards and shows its white undertail feathers. It makes an explosive bubbling sound as well as various shrieks and groans.

The small **Black Crake** is another bird of the shallows and reed fringes, also with an explosive call. The **African Rail** is reluctant to show itself, but its shrill calls show it to be fairly common among the reeds. The slightest disturbance will send it back into cover.

Grebes belong to a different family from rails and crakes. They swim on the same waters as ducks, but are seldom seen out of water or flying (which they do at night). Their legs are set well back on the body for optimal underwater propulsion. When a grebe is at its floating nest, it shuffles about, mostly resting its breast on the nest.

The **Little Grebe**, the smallest common swimming bird on inland waters, is generally known as the **Dabchick**. It has two cousins – the **Black-necked Grebe**, common in the western parts of the region, and the larger **Great Crested Grebe**, a widespread and very striking bird which is nowhere common and spends most of its time away from the shoreline. The Little Grebe dives underwater to feed (usually just when you are looking at it) and then pops up again in a different place. Its call is a shrill descending trill. The Great Crested Grebe also dives for its food and prefers fairly deep water.

▲ In breeding plumage, the **Little Grebe** (length 20 cm) has a chestnut-brown patch on the side of its head and neck and a cream spot at the base of its bill.

▲ The 'horned' head-crest of the stately **Great Crested Grebe** (length 50 cm) are unmistakable.

Notes

- Rails differ from ducks in important ways. They do not have the flattened bill and many have frontal shields on their foreheads. They do not have webbed feet like ducks, but those that swim a lot may have toe-flanges like those of grebes.
- With the possible exception of coots, rails do not swim in flocks. They feed mostly on vegetation as well as some insects and tadpoles.

Red-chested Flufftail   Buff-spotted Flufftail   Black-necked Grebe

Storks

The **Saddle-billed Stork** (length 145 cm) is black and white with very long legs and a heavy, red-and-black, saddle-topped bill. Males are told by dark eyes and yellow wattles; females have yellow eyes and no wattles.

Like most storks, the **Yellow-billed Stork** flies with neck and legs outstretched.

SOME LESS COMMON SOUTHERN AFRICAN STORKS

Open-billed Stork   Black Stork   Woolly-necked Stork

Storks are large to very large, long-legged, heavy-billed birds that feed in water or grasslands. Some storks have brightly coloured bills and legs, but most are black and white or just blackish. The neck is usually of medium length, but a few species have a long neck. Storks feed by day; some fish, others forage in the veld for locusts and grasshoppers. They are silent birds although pairs may greet each other at the nest by clapping their bills. Most storks feed and move in flocks. Only the Black Stork and Saddle-billed Stork are solitary, sometimes moving in groups of two or three.

Resident storks (Yellow-billed, Saddle-billed, Black, Woolly-necked, Open-billed and Marabou) are to be seen feeding in rivers in bushveld. Woolly-necked as well as Open-billed storks are nomadic and often move over fairly long distances to new feeding grounds. The Saddle-billed Stork and Marabou Stork are southern Africa's largest storks.

The **Saddle-billed Stork** is always found in wetlands and is quite unmistakable at rest or in flight, its colourful bill topped with a yellow 'saddle'. The even larger **Marabou Stork** feeds in wetlands or in big game country, where it will

The resident **Yellow-billed Stork** (length 97 cm) may be seen at inland waters in bushveld.

scavenge with vultures. It even feeds at rubbish tips. Unlike most other storks, it tucks its head into its shoulders (like a heron) when it flies. The sausage-like appendage at the base of the neck can be inflated like a balloon to radiate body heat in hot weather.

The largest bird to migrate annually to Africa from its breeding grounds in Europe is the **White Stork**, which has all-white plumage except for black flight feathers. The birds arrive in Africa in thousands around October, eventually reaching southern Africa in November. Until their return migration about five months later, flocks – often large – feed on locusts and other pests in farmlands and bushveld. A small population of White Storks happens to be resident at the Cape.

Another November arrival, this time from Ethiopia and the Sudan, is the tawny-billed, blue-faced, pink-legged **Abdim's Stork**, a smaller species which often feeds in mixed flocks with White Storks through the summer months.

The **White Stork** (length 117 cm), a common non-breeding summer visitor, has a bright red bill and legs.

Abdim's Stork (length 76 cm), another summer visitor, may be seen in farmlands, often in large flocks.

The **Marabou Stork** (length 152 cm) has a massive tawny-coloured bill, grey upperparts, white underparts and grey legs stained white. Its head and neck are bald except for a few hairs.

Notes

- Initially, storks may be confused with herons (see pages 54–55). Storks are more colourful and more heavily built than herons, have heavier bills and are usually seen in flocks. When breeding, they do not have plumes on the head and body like herons and their bills and bare facial-skin do not change colour.
- Most storks fly with the neck extended and, unlike herons, soar to great heights in rising warm air (thermals) when they are travelling.

Widows & bishops

Br ♂

N-Br ♂

Widows and bishops differ most markedly from other weavers in the family in that breeding males develop predominantly black plumage in summer. At this time some widows also acquire long tails. Male bishops retain their normal tails but have longer than usual red or yellow body feathers. Males perform flight displays over their nesting territories, the widows displaying their long tails and the bishops their puffed-out plumage, which creates an impression of larger size.

Female widows and bishops are brownish, pale below and darker above with dark streaks, and are difficult to identify to species when not with males. Males in non-breeding plumage are similar to females, but some retain traces of their breeding colours on shoulder or rump. In most species the song is of a rasping or swizzling nature. Widows and bishops are highly gregarious birds when not breeding and form mixed nomadic flocks in farmlands.

The most spectacular display flight is that of the breeding male **Long-tailed Widow**. Because of its size and voluminous tail, it is visible at a distance as it patrols its territory in low flight with exaggerated wing actions. The range of this widow is restricted to grasslands and farmlands in the coastal region between Port Elizabeth and Durban and northward in a broad band to a latitude of about 24 degrees.

◀ When perched, the **Long-tailed Widow** (length 19–60 cm) shows its scarlet-and-cream wing-patches which, with the grey bill, are retained by males in non-breeding plumage.

♀

A male **White-winged Widow** ▶
(length 15–19 cm)
in display.

SOME LESS COMMON SOUTHERN AFRICAN WIDOWS AND BISHOPS

Red-shouldered Widow

Yellow-rumped Widow

Yellow-backed Widow

Fire-crowned Bishop

The smaller **Red-collared Widow** male also makes flight displays, but of a shorter duration, and displays from a perch while calling. It has a wider easterly distribution than the Long-tailed Widow and is mostly seen on the fringes of old cultivations and on hillsides with scattered trees.

The shorter-tailed **White-winged Widow** with its white-and-yellow wing-patches also has an easterly distribution but is absent from Mozambique. It prefers damp localities with rank grass, often in otherwise dry areas. The male displays with fanned tail and a twittering call from a perch. In flight its white and yellow wing-markings flash conspicuously.

The male **Red Bishop** is well known for its brilliant red-and-black breeding plumage and display flights over reedbeds in summer. It is highly water-associated when breeding, its call a continuous 'zik zik zik zayzayzayzay . . .'

Equally spectacular in display, if less frequently seen, is the smaller **Golden Bishop**. It prefers moist grasslands, rank grass and sedges on the fringes of streams and dams, and growing crops. The male Golden Bishop flies to and fro over its nest sites displaying with rapidly beating wings and fully fluffed crown and rump, looking like a large, yellow bumble-bee. At other times of year, Golden and Red bishops form large, mixed, nomadic flocks.

W. Tarboton

Without a full frontal view, the narrow red collar of the male **Red-collared Widow** (length 15–40 cm) may be difficult to see.

When its breeding plumage is not puffed up in display, the male **Golden Bishop** (length 12 cm) can appear quite small.

Female **Golden Bishops** resemble males that are not in breeding plumage.

In display the male **Red Bishop** (length 14 cm) either perches with fully fluffed plumage on a reed near the nest site or patrols in short flights with fast-flapping wings and puffed plumage.

Cranes

Cranes are large, long-legged, long-necked terrestrial birds that (unlike storks) have short bills and are quite vocal. Pairs or groups indulge in elaborate dances, leaping and wheeling with wings raised and tossing bits of grass in the air – thought to be an expression of group excitement rather than courtship. Like storks, cranes fly with head, neck and legs outstretched. They are moderately gregarious, gathering in family or larger groups and frequenting open grasslands and wetlands away from human activity. Male cranes are a little larger than females.

The three endemic species described here have suffered serious population reductions in South Africa in recent years and, in different degrees, are considered to be endangered. Their decline is attributed to wetland habitat loss and to collisions with power lines, poisoning, chick-theft for the wild bird trade, and other forms of human interference. Cranes should be admired but left undisturbed wherever they are seen if populations are to increase beyond their present dangerously low levels.

The largest of our cranes is the stately and 'Critically Endangered' **Wattled Crane.** It is estimated that there are 230 individuals in South Africa, Lesotho and Swaziland. The call of this large and majestic bird is a trumpeting and far-carrying 'horaank'. The largest population of

▲
The **Wattled Crane** (length 120 cm) has grey upperparts and trailing inner wing-feathers, a white body and neck and a grey-capped head. It has long, horn-coloured legs.

▲
A deep red, fleshy covering extends from the base of the Wattled Crane's bill onto its long, white, feathered wattles.

The **Grey Crowned Crane** (length 105 cm) ▶ has a black head with white facial-patch, red-tipped wattles, blackish bill and legs, and a predominantly grey body.

Wattled Cranes is found in the Okavango Delta in northern Botswana (where aerial surveys suggest a population of 1 219 birds).

The **Blue Crane** is found in the eastern regions of southern Africa in hilly grassland, moist valleys, karoo and, especially, in the Cape fynbos biome. There is also a small isolated population in the area of the Etosha Pan, Namibia. The total population at present is about 21 000 individuals. The call of the Blue Crane is a rattling, nasal 'kraaaarrk'.

The striking **Crowned Crane** (re-named the **Grey Crowned Crane**), easily identified by its bushy crown of golden feathers, is the same size as the Blue Crane and is also categorized 'Vulnerable', the total South African population now fewer than 3 000 individuals. Its call is a trumpeting 'mahem' (its Afrikaans name). Its main area of distribution is the high-rainfall regions of the eastern parts of South Africa, chiefly the Eastern Cape and the southern and midland regions of KwaZulu-Natal. Populations also occur in Zimbabwe and Mozambique. Grey Crowned Cranes inhabit grassland and farmland as well as marshy areas at both high and low altitudes.

When they are not breeding, cranes are normally gregarious. Where conditions are favourable, the number of birds in a flock may be in the hundreds. Nowadays, however, the birds are more often seen in smaller gatherings. Where possible, they prefer to spend the night standing in water or on a small island, safe from nocturnal predators. They seldom, if ever, perch in trees.

Cranes are opportunistic feeders on vegetable matter as well as insects, reptiles, frogs and small mammals.

Entirely blue-grey except for a white crown on its bulbous head, the **Blue Crane** (length 105 cm) has an orange-horn bill and horn-coloured legs. Its trailing inner-wing feathers look like a long tail.

Although they prefer to walk, **Wattled Cranes** are capable of powerful and sustained flight.

Notes

- Since the problem of bird collisions with high-voltage power lines was identified some years ago Eskom (Electricity Supply Commission) has gone to great lengths to modify its lines to make them more visible to large flying birds.
- The South African Crane Foundation undertakes the rearing of young cranes in captivity for their eventual release in the wild. As cranes lay two eggs and normally raise only one, the second egg is removed for hand-rearing.
- Most cranes are monogamous and pair for life. They have a low reproduction rate, nesting on the ground in open areas and incubating their eggs for 30–40 days. The young fledge at about four months of age, but stay with their parents for up to 10 months.

Common bee-eaters

N. Myburgh

▲
The yellow throat of the **European Bee-eater** (length 25–29 cm) is separated from its blue underparts by a narrow black collar.

The **White-fronted Bee-eater** (length ▶ 22–24 cm) has green upperparts except for a cinnamon-brown nape that extends around the neck to the entire underparts. Its throat is crimson and its vent blue.

Bee-eaters are brightly coloured, specialized aerial feeders that are among our most beautiful birds. They have quite sharply tapered wings and fly with much twisting and turning in pursuit of prey. Average length is 22–26 cm, the exception in our region being the 17-cm Little Bee-eater while some of the larger species with extended tail-shafts may reach 38 cm. All bee-eaters have a decurved black bill, short black legs and dark brown eyes set in a black mask extending from the base of the bill to the ear coverts. The sexes are alike.

Bee-eaters nest in long tunnels that they excavate in banks, occasionally in the ground. They are birds of open woodland and riverine bush and catch various flying insects in addition to venomous bees, their preferred diet. They hunt from the ground (or a perch or bush) or while flying. The four species most likely to be encountered are Little, White-fronted, European (or Golden-backed) and Carmine bee-eaters.

SOME LESS COMMON SOUTHERN AFRICAN BEE-EATERS

Böhm's Bee-eater   Swallow-tailed Bee-eater   Olive Bee-eater   Blue-cheeked Bee-eater

The **European** or **Golden-backed Bee-eater** is normally seen in flocks. It has a chestnut-brown rear crown and mantle over a golden-yellow back, its forehead ('front') blue and uppertail green. In flight the back contrasts sharply with the brown inner and blue-green outer wings. Individuals in the air call a distinctive 'quilp'. These bee-eaters breed in Europe, but also in North Africa, Namibia, the Cape (including the Northern Cape) and the Free State. The alternative and more descriptive name 'Golden-backed' is thus more accurate than 'European' Bee-eater.

The **Little Bee-eater** (one of the smallest species in the family) normally occurs in small groups of two to six birds in open scrub or low-bush terrain, often near a river. The birds forage in repeated sallies from a low perch. The larger **White-fronted Bee-eater**, so named for its white forehead and chin, is very much a riverside species, breeding and roosting in flocks in river-bank colonies.

The largest bee-eater in our region is the **Carmine Bee-eater**, which breeds in Botswana, Zimbabwe and to the north and visits South Africa as a post-breeding visitor in mid-summer. Its flight call is 'terk terk'. Look for it in the Limpopo Province and Kruger National Park. Flocks are very large and include many young birds of the season. These juveniles are much duller in colour than the adults and usually lack the long tail-shafts.

G. Lockwood

The predominantly carmine-red **Carmine Bee-eater** (length 33–38 cm), often seen in mid-summer in the Kruger National Park, is unmistakable with its long tail-shafts and blue crown and vent.

Notes

- When a bee-eater returns to its perch with a venomous bee, it rubs off the sting against the perch and squeezes the bee's abdomen to eject the venom before swallowing the insect.
- European Bee-eaters (and probably others that regularly feed during prolonged flight) appear to be able to de-venom a worker bee without having to settle. They can also differentiate between a non-venomous drone and a worker and will select the venomous worker in preference to the drone.
- In an active Carmine Bee-eater breeding colony, which was observed for two hours, parent birds feeding nestlings were not seen to select any venomous insects. Only dragon-flies, damselflies, large dung beetles and grasshoppers were taken into the burrows.

N. Myburgh

The **Little Bee-eater** (length 17 cm) has entirely green upperparts, a yellow throat and cinnamon underparts surmounted by a black 'bib'.

Common hornbills

G. Lockwood

Hornbills are not related to toucans. They belong to Africa and the East; toucans are found only in the Americas. Ten species of hornbill are found in southern Africa and all but one lead mostly arboreal lives. The exception is the huge, mainly terrestrial Southern Ground Hornbill.

All hornbills are frugivorous and insectivorous and feed on the ground and in trees. African Grey, Southern Yellow-billed and Red-billed hornbills are the most common, occurring through much of the northern bushveld region. They enter towns only in country districts. The bills of hornbills are light and largely hollow, functioning as sound boxes that give added resonance to their calls.

In the **African Grey Hornbill** the sexes are slightly different, both with a prominent white eyebrow above a dark eye, and dark grey head and upperparts with cream-edged wing-feathers in contrast to the white underparts. The bird

▲ A male **African Grey Hornbill** (length 43–48 cm) showing the casque on the upper mandible of its black bill with cream side-patch. Females have shorter bills and a cream casque and upper mandible.

The **Red-billed Hornbill** (length 42–50 cm) ▶ has a more pointed bill than the Southern Yellow-billed Hornbill.

SOME LESS COMMON SOUTHERN AFRICAN HORNBILLS

Crowned Hornbill   Monteiro's Hornbill   Bradfield's Hornbill   Trumpeter Hornbill

delivers a high-pitched piping while pointing its bill skywards. The African Grey Hornbill is the most arboreal of the three common species described here.

The **Red-billed Hornbill** and **Southern Yellow-billed Hornbill** are easily recognized by bill colour and their superficially similar, black-and-white checkered upper plumage. The two species have remarkably similar calls, a lengthy series of 'wak wak wak wak . . .' sounds. The sexes in both are very alike.

The huge **Southern Ground Hornbill** is usually seen in family groups of between four to ten in eastern and northern bushveld regions. The birds forage together and can overpower many small creatures on the ground with jabs of their heavy bills. They fly to roost at night in large trees, revealing white wing-feathers. The call, heard mostly at dawn, is a deep and far-carrying booming. There has been an alarming decrease in the numbers of Southern Ground Hornbills in recent years as a result of tree felling and other environmental changes, as well as the use of their body parts in traditional medicine.

▲ The adult **Southern Ground Hornbill** (length 90 cm) is entirely black except for bright red facial skin and throat-pouch (yellow in immature birds). Females have a central blue patch as well.

◄ The **Southern Yellow-billed Hornbill** (length 48–60 cm) has a deeper bill than the similar Red-billed Hornbill. The male is seen perched (left) and (above) feeding its mate in the sealed nest.

Notes

- When she nests, a female hornbill uses mud and droppings to seal herself into a tree cavity with the help of her mate. She leaves only a small slit into which food can be passed. While incubating the eggs she depends on her mate to feed her as she undergoes a complete moult of her flight feathers and is temporarily flightless.
- Ground hornbills nest in very large tree holes like those created when branches fall from large trees. Felling of these old trees creates a shortage of suitable nest sites. Ground hornbills do not seal their nest cavities.

Damara Hornbill   Silvery-cheeked Hornbill

Drongoes & similar black birds

W. Tarboton

The **Fork-tailed Drongo** (length 25 cm) has a distinctly forked tail which accounts for a good part of its total length. It has dark brown eyes.

The juvenile **Fork-tailed** Drongo is a dull brown and, initially, lacks the forked tail.

Juv

Although not exactly square, the tip of the tail of the **Square-tailed Drongo** (length 19 cm) has only a shallow fork. The Square-tailed also differs from the Fork-tailed in the colour of its eyes.

Because these four black birds are confusingly similar and easily misidentified, they are best shown together for ease of comparison.

The **Fork-tailed Drongo** is a distinctive and common bushveld and woodland bird. Novice birders will soon hear the name bandied about, probably long before they encounter the bird. The width of the distinctively forked tail (a diagnostic feature) is created by the outward splay of the two outermost feathers. This bird is, moreover, conspicuous and noisy, and often imitates the sounds made by other species.

You will soon come to recognize the Fork-tailed Drongo, but beware! Its smaller cousin, the **Square-tailed Drongo**, is also black and noisy and has splayed outer tail-feathers. However, the Square-tailed Drongo's eyes are wine-red and its tail has a very shallow fork. Of more importance, perhaps, it is a bird of evergreen forests and not of the bushveld.

Now take a look at the **Black Flycatcher** which shares the same bushveld habitat as the Fork-tailed Drongo but is more slender and has a straight tail without the outward splaying and only a very small central indent at the tip. In

H. Chittenden

contrast with the noisy drongoes, this is a very quiet bird, merely uttering an occasional soft 'swee'. Like the drongoes, it is a still-hunter and perches openly on the side of a tree.

Yet another black bird is the male **Black Cuckooshrike**, a species that is quite unrelated to the others mentioned here. The male bird may be entirely black or have a distinctive yellow 'shoulder' or carpal joint, in which case identification should not be too difficult. In the entirely black morph, meanwhile, careful scrutiny will reveal a straight tail with a rounded tip. Even closer scrutiny and a good view of the head reveals a clear orange-yellow gape, present in both sexes and reminiscent of a fledgling bird. The Black Cuckooshrike is found in broad-leaved woodland. It is a sluggish leaf-gleaner and spends much time in the tree canopy.

The tip of the tail of the **Black Flycatcher** (length 20–22 cm) shows a very small central indent, not a fork.

In the **Black Cuckooshrike** (length 22 cm) the small yellow carpal patch in the plumage of many males is completely absent in the entirely black form (on the right).

The strikingly different female **Black Cuckooshrike** has colourful, cuckoo-like plumage.

Notes

- The Fork-tailed Drongo is either very bold or very foolhardy for it does not hesitate to attack passing birds of prey, even pecking at eagles to help them on their way.
- The Square-tailed Drongo is usually the first bird to be heard on entering a forest. It maintains a noisy chatter until the intruder leaves.
- The name 'cuckooshrike' is derived from the cuckoo-like plumage patterns of some species, certainly the case in the female Black Cuckooshrike.

Flycatchers & batises

W. Tarboton

A pair of **African Paradise Flycatchers** at the nest, the male (length 41 cm) with long tail-plumes. Both sexes have an orange-brown or chestnut back, wings and tail, blue-grey crested head and breast, and a bright blue bill and eye-rings.

The **Spotted Flycatcher** (length 14–15 cm) has ▶ more streaking than 'spots' on its breast and can be told also by the dark streaks on its head.

Flycatchers catch most small non-venomous insects as well as flies. They are small to medium-size (length 11–22 cm), the exception being the male Paradise Flycatcher with its very long tail. Plumage varies from bright and striking to very drab. All flycatchers have a shortish, slender bill, stiff rictal bristles projecting from the base of the bill, and slender, blackish legs. Their bill shape and the small size of many species may initially cause them to be confused with some birds in the warbler group. The most frequently seen, according to distribution and habitat preference, are Paradise, Marico and Fiscal flycatchers and the Chin-spot Batis and Cape Batis, especially during the summer months.

Flycatchers may be divided into three groups according to hunting technique:

Hawkers (e.g. Paradise, Blue-grey and Black flycatchers) dart out from a perch in a tree and seize passing insects in brief aerial sallies, often with complicated acrobatics. The prey is snapped up with an audible clap of the bill and the bird returns to its perch to eat it.

W. Tarboton

SOME LESS COMMON SOUTHERN AFRICAN FLYCATCHERS

| Dusky Flycatcher | Pallid Flycatcher | Fan-tailed Flycatcher | Blue-grey Flycatcher | Chat Flycatcher |

Still-hunters (e.g. Spotted, Fiscal, Dusky, Pallid, Marico and Chat flycatchers) perch on top of a tree or bush, or on a side branch or fence, and watch the ground for insect movement. They fly down to seize insect prey and return to the perch to consume it.

Canopy-foragers and *leaf-gleaners* (e.g. Wattle-eyed, White-tailed, Fan-tailed, Fairy and Livingstone's flycatchers and the five members of the batis group) inspect branches and leaves in the tree or bush canopy for aphids, caterpillars, and other insects. They occasionally fly out in pursuit of an insect that has been disturbed.

The **African Paradise Flycatcher** breeds in summer in much of southern Africa other than the arid western parts; its non-breeding range is confined to low-altitude eastern regions. Like the still-hunting **Spotted Flycatcher**, a non-breeding summer visitor from Europe, the bird may be seen in well-wooded gardens and parks in many towns. The endemic black-and-white **Fiscal Flycatcher** is a frequent visitor to gardens in many parts of the region.

The batis group of flycatchers have mixed russet, grey, black and white plumage, and vary in size from 10–12 cm. The **Cape Batis**, the most boldly marked of the batises in southern and eastern forests, normally occurs in groups of five or six birds. The **Chin-spot Batis** is the most widespread, in pairs, in bushveld regions. Its call is three descending notes which resemble the words 'three-blind-mice'.

The **Fiscal Flycatcher** (length 17–20 cm) still-hunts from its perch on a branch or post.

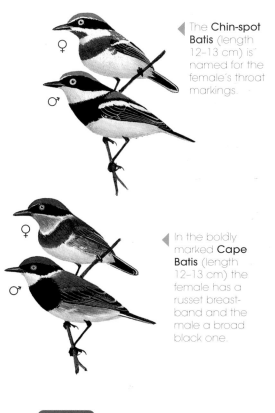

The **Chin-spot Batis** (length 12–13 cm) is named for the female's throat markings.

In the boldly marked **Cape Batis** (length 12–13 cm) the female has a russet breast-band and the male a broad black one.

The distinctive **Marico Flycatcher** (length 18 cm) with its conspicuous white underparts is found mostly in western parts of the region.

W. Tarboton

Pririt Batis   Fairy Flycatcher   Wattle-eyed Flycatcher

Notes

- When identifying flycatchers remember that the Blue-mantled, White-tailed and Livingstone's flycatchers are found only in evergreen forests while the Dusky Flycatcher frequents the fringes of forests.
- The Fiscal Flycatcher differs from the Fiscal Shrike (see pages 40–41) in that it has a slender bill and a white wing-bar that does not reach its shoulder.

Rollers

▲
The well-known **Lilac-breasted Roller** (length 36 cm) has elongated outer tail-feathers and occurs less seasonally than the European Roller.

Rollers are colourful birds in which some species perform noisy courtship flights such as the Lilac-breasted Roller's steep rise followed by an aerial roll and erratic, rocking descent. Southern Africa is home to five rollers, all around 36 cm in length. The Purple Roller and Broad-billed Roller are the less common species.

Rollers are stout-bodied with a short neck, large head and a tail of medium length, some with extended outer tail feathers. Their bills are mostly robust with slightly hooked tips, their legs shortish but strong. Their body plumage features deep reds, blues or purples and the flight feathers are a radiant, electric-blue, striking when the bird is in the air. The sexes are similar.

Most rollers are still-hunters, catching large insects and spiders from a prominent tree perch and seizing small reptiles on the ground. Their preferred habitat is savanna woodland and thornveld. They have harsh, rasping calls.

The widespread and very aptly named **Lilac-breasted Roller** is the best known roller in southern Africa. The **European Roller** is similar in appearance, but lacks the lilac breast. It is more seasonal in occurrence – a mid-summer, non-breeding visitor – and observations of it are mostly scattered. The **Racket-tailed Roller** is similar in appearance to these two rollers but

G. Lockwood

▲▶
Although similar to the Lilac-breasted Roller, the **European Roller** (length 30–31 cm) is entirely turquoise-blue from head to underparts and has a square tail.

with additional extended outer tail feathers. It is more often seen in miombo woodland in Zimbabwe than south of the Limpopo. These three rollers are alike in behaviour.

The **Purple Roller** is a larger, more heavily built bird than the other southern African rollers. In comparison with the others, it is rather sluggish although well up to the aerial roll in display.

The **Broad-billed Roller**, the smallest of the group, is an intra-Africa migrant that visits and breeds in the region only in summer. It is an aerial hunter, catching insects in rapid sallies from high up in a tree. It favours palms where these occur and also the vicinity of rivers and wetlands. Largely crepuscular in habit, it often performs late into the evening and engages in noisy and aggressive pursuit of other birds. Its voice is a variety of harsh cackles and croaks.

G. Lockwood

▲
The **Broad-billed Roller** (length 27 cm) is told by its cinnamon upperparts, purple head and body and broad yellow bill.

▲
The **Purple Roller** (length 36–40 cm) has a purple-red body streaked white. Its flight feathers are deep blue and its forehead whitish, extending to a distinct eyebrow.

▲
The **Racket-tailed Roller** (length 36 cm) has distinctive, spatulate outer tail feathers. It is often seen in association with baobab trees, especially in Zimbabwe.

Notes

- All five rollers are to be found in the Kruger National Park. With the exception of the Racket-tailed Roller, they are easily seen. They breed in southern Africa in summer, using natural holes in trees or, occasionally, holes in cliffs and termite mounds.

Bush shrikes & boubou shrikes

Unlike true shrikes (see pages 40–41), bush shrikes are colourful and have attractive calls. Their upperparts are mostly olive-green and grey, the underparts yellow, orange or red, and they often have black masks or breast-bands. The sexes are closely similar. The related boubous are black and white and (in one species) black and crimson, with ringing ventriloquil calls that are rendered in very variable duets.

Bush shrikes are mostly evasive birds that are found in bushveld or forest. However, the near-endemic **Bokmakierie** is a common garden bird, well known for its cheerful calls, usually delivered as a duet, one sex answering the other. The calls are the source of the name 'bok-makiri' – or 'kok-o-vik' or 'bok bok-chit' and other variations.

The little **Orange-breasted Bush Shrike** frequents dense bushveld, riverine and coastal thickets in the mid-stratum where it is not secretive but is often difficult to locate, even while calling its tantalizing 'poo-poo-poo-poooooo' or 'pipit-eeez, pipit-eeez'. A much larger bird in the same habitat and with very similar colouring is the beautiful **Grey-headed Bush Shrike** or 'Spookvoel', which is best known for its haunting, highly ventriloquil 'hoooooooooooooop'.

The well-known **Bokmakierie** (length 23 cm) has bright yellow underparts and a conspicuous black breast-band (gorget).

The **Grey-headed Bush Shrike** (length 25–27 cm) has yellow eyes and a heavy hooked bill. It has the unattractive habit of raiding other birds' nests and eating their young.

LESS COMMON SOUTHERN AFRICAN BUSH SHRIKES

Olive Bush Shrike

Gorgeous Bush Shrike

Black-fronted Bush Shrike

This bush shrike is not a shy bird, but it is always on the move and sometimes difficult to find since one does not know where its call is coming from.

The three less common bush shrikes shown at the bottom of the page are rather secretive species, two of which (Olive and Black-fronted) occur in the indigenous evergreen eastern forests where they are difficult to locate although very vocal. The Gorgeous Bush Shrike frequents dense coastal bush, valley bush (thicket) and riverine forests, its tantalizing call a liquid and rapidly delivered 'kong-kong-quoit'.

There are four boubou shrikes in the region and three of them – Southern Boubou, Swamp Boubou (which occurs mostly in the Okavango Delta) and Tropical Boubou (found mostly in Zimbabwe) – are almost identical: black above and beneath the eye and white or buffy-white below with a bold white wingbar. The **Southern Boubou** frequents the lower stratum of the bush and, to a large extent, forages on the ground. It is quite common in urban areas, calling in ringing duets, the first bird calling 'ko-ko' replied to by 'kweet' or 'boo-boo' replied to by 'whe-oo' or a liquid-sounding 'phooweeol' replied to by 'hueee' or 'churr'. The notes are delivered so rapidly as to sound like a single bird calling.

The fourth species and odd man out is the very striking **Crimson-breasted Boubou**, which is also called the **Crimson-breasted Shrike**. This bird's underparts are entirely crimson in colour.

W. Tarboton

The **Orange-breasted Bush Shrike** (length 18–19 cm), seen here at its nest, has yellow underparts, a black mask and orange breast. The sexes are alike.

◀ A rare yellow morph of the **Crimson-breasted Boubou**.

W. Tarboton

In the **Southern Boubou** (length 23 cm) the white underparts are variably washed with cinnamon especially towards the tail.

W. Tarboton

The **Crimson-breasted Boubou** (length 22–23 cm) is a bird of acacia thornveld, its rapid rasping 'qui-quip-chiri' call delivered as a duet between the sexes.

Tchagras & helmet shrikes

Tchagra shrikes are heavy-billed birds, with distinctive calls. They frequent the lower stratum of their habitat, even foraging on the ground. Of the four southern African tchagra shrikes, three have chestnut-brown wings, a tawny mantle, dusky white underparts, bold black eye-stripe and either a black or brown crown (a diagnostic feature). The fourth, the Marsh Tchagra, is highly localized, occurring in marshy regions in eastern Zimbabwe and Mozambique. It differs from other tchagras in that it has a black cap and a rust wash on its underparts.

The **Southern Tchagra** is common but secretive. It lives in dense thickets and coastal bush, ranging from the southern Cape coast to KwaZulu-Natal and, sparsely, into the northern Drakensberg. It is heard more often than seen, its in-flight call a loud rattling followed by a descending 'chechechechetewtewtew'.

The **Black-crowned Tchagra** is common in woodland, thornveld and coastal bush mainly in north-eastern regions. Its whistled call is a rather ponderous, flat-sounding 'cheer-tcharee, trichi-

▲
The **Southern Tchagra** (length 21–23 cm) is distinguished from the similar but smaller Brown-crowned Tchagra by its plain brown crown without black edges and by dusky white underparts.

H. Chittenden

▲
When the crown of the **Brown-crowned Tchagra** (length 19 cm) cannot be seen, the bird can be told by its pale mantle and sides of neck.

H. Chittenden

▲
In the **Black-crowned Tchagra** (length 21–23 cm) the tawny colour of the mantle extends to the sides of the head and neck.

cheer-tcharoo, cheeree cheeroo'. It may easily be confused with the smaller **Brown-crowned** (or **Three-streaked**) **Tchagra**, which is found in much the same localities and habitats but has a wider range to the west. The brown crown of the Brown-crowned Tchagra is edged black, and it has a distinctive 'tui tui tui tui tui . . .' call uttered in a descending cadence while the bird planes down from above tree height.

Helmet shrikes are small, highly social, insectivorous, nomadic birds characterized by a forward-projecting head-crest. There are three species in southern Africa, the smallest of which – the rare **Chestnut-fronted Helmet Shrike** – is confined to eastern Zimbabwe and Mozambique, where it is sparsely distributed.

Parties of **White Helmet Shrikes** are fairly common in bushveld and woodland regions. With their pied plumage they look like a flock of butterflies as they flap their way over the bushes. These birds maintain a constant, subdued chattering which involves whirring sounds and bill-snapping. The **Red-billed Helmet Shrike** occurs in the riverine forests of broadleaved woodland, where parties frequent the tree canopies. They sometimes forage with White Helmet Shrikes, their calls sounding much alike.

N. Myburgh

▲ A **White Helmet Shrike** on its nest, which is very likely the work of several birds in the group.

▲ The yellow legs and eye-wattles, grey crest and short black bill of the **White Helmet Shrike** (length 20 cm) are visible at close range.

▲ The **Red-billed Helmet Shrike** (length 22 cm) is told by its mostly black plumage (vent and tail-tips white) and its red bill, eye-wattles and legs.

▲ The rare **Chestnut-fronted Helmet Shrike** (length 19 cm) has a diagnostic chestnut forehead and red bill and legs.

Notes

- Helmet shrikes form family groups of six to twelve birds. The birds feed and roost together and, when breeding, share nest-building and chick-feeding duties. This kind of social behaviour is seen in other nomadic species.

Turacos & go-away birds

The alternative names 'turaco' and 'go-away' are preferable to 'lourie', a name which it appears was wrongly applied by early Dutch travellers who took the red-winged 'Knysna Lourie' to be a parrot and related, thus, to the lories and lorikeets they knew from the East. The southern African birds are a purely African family and are not remotely related to parrots. The scientific name for the genus, *Tauraco* (modified in English to 'turaco'), derives from the red pigment (turacine) in the wings. Those birds that lack red wings are known as go-away birds.

The well-known and admired **Knysna Turaco** and its races (Livingstone's and Schalow's turacos) are birds of evergreen forests, usually first noticed by a flash of crimson as they fly past or the sound of their 'kawk kawk kawk' call. The **Purple-crested Turaco** is a bird of large lowland riverine forests or dense woodland, its hidden presence revealed by its 'kok-kok-kok-kok . . .' call. These birds are fairly common in their favoured habitats.

The common and widespread **Grey Go-away Bird**, long regarded as a bushveld species, is now a common garden bird in regions it did not previously inhabit. This entirely grey bird with erect head-crest visits bird tables for handouts of soft fruits. It can become very tolerant of human activity.

▲ The **Knysna Turaco** (length 47 cm) and its races – Livingstone's Turaco (b) and Schalow's Turaco (c) – differ mainly in the length of the head crest.

The 'go-wayyy . . .' call of the **Grey Go-away Bird** (length 47–50 cm) can be a source of much amusement. ▶

N. Myburgh

▲ Common in woodland, the **Purple-crested Turaco** (length 47 cm) is more often heard than seen.

Notes

- Ross's Turaco (Lourie) is illustrated in *Newman's Birds of Southern Africa* based on a single vagrant shot in the Okavango Delta some 30 years ago. Subsequent sightings in Sandton (Johannesburg) refer to feral Violet Turacos from West Africa that were released or escaped from captivity.

Babblers

Babblers are thrush-like terrestrial birds of gregarious habits with very similar babbling calls, some higher pitched than others. They sound like an excited cackling, uttered by the entire group. There are five species in southern Africa, found in mixed bushveld and riverine woodland where they forage mostly in the lower stratum. All have a northern or north-westerly distribution.

All babblers have black bills and legs and orange or pale yellow eyes, some with red eye surrounds. Two species are predominantly white and three are mostly brownish. Some are confusingly similar in appearance. The sexes are alike.

The **Arrow-marked Babbler** is the most common and widespread babbler in the region. Another common but localized species is the **Southern White-rumped (or Hartlaub's) Babbler**, well named for its appearance. It is found in the Okavango Delta and the adjacent wetlands. The very distinctive **Southern Pied Babbler** is a bird of the drier western regions.

The calls of babblers may be confused with those of Red-billed Woodhoopoes, but are more mechanical sounding.

The **Southern Pied Babbler** (length 26 cm) is a quite unmistakable, almost entirely white bird.

The white rump and vent of the **Southern White-rumped Babbler** (length 26 cm) are highly distinctive in the field, as is the scaly appearance of its plumage. It has red eyes.

The **Arrow-marked Babbler** (length 23–25 cm) is named for the white markings on its upperparts. It has orange eyes with red rims.

SOME LESS COMMON SOUTHERN AFRICAN BABBLERS

Black-lored Babbler   Bare-cheeked Babbler

Woodpeckers & Wryneck

Woodpeckers are unobtrusive but widespread. Our four most common arboreal species are best identified by checking their underparts for streaks, spots or bands. Head- and facial-markings are also helpful, but can prove confusing since the sexes differ. All four species have shortish, black, dagger-like bills, dark eyes and blackish legs. Woodpeckers are usually located by the sound of their pecking.

The largest of the common woodpeckers is the **Bearded Woodpecker**, told by grey underparts with fine, horizontal white bars. Both sexes have large, heavy bills, the throat and face white, separated by a bold black malar-stripe and earpatch. The call is a loud 'wickwickwickwick' but the male also indulges in loud, early-morning territorial drumming on a hollow branch. The sound is a far-carrying 'trrrrrr-taptaptaptap' like a drum-roll. The Bearded Woodpecker occurs in mature woodland with well-spaced trees.

Both sexes of the **Bearded Woodpecker** (length 23–25 cm) have a black forehead speckled white and banded underparts. The male has a red central crown, the female a black crown which extends to the hind-neck.

In the **Golden-tailed Woodpecker** (length 20–23 cm) the male has a red moustachial-stripe, black-speckled red crown and clear red nape. In the female both moustachial-stripe and crown are black, speckled white, and the nape red.

SOME LESS COMMON SOUTHERN AFRICAN WOODPECKERS

| Ground Woodpecker | Little Spotted Woodpecker | Speckle-throated Woodpecker | Knysna Woodpecker | Olive Woodpecker |

As all arboreal woodpeckers have golden tails. the name of the **Golden-tailed Woodpecker** is not an identification feature. Its underparts are black-streaked but rather less densely – except for the throat – than those of the Cardinal Woodpecker. The Golden-tailed Woodpecker has a far-carrying and distinctive nasal 'waaaaa' call which it utters frequently.

The **Cardinal Woodpecker** is the smallest of the common woodpeckers, absent only in treeless parts of the region. Both sexes have a brown forehead, well-streaked underparts and black malar-stripe. They call a rapid, high-pitched 'kekekekekek' which is repeated by birds of either sex. This woodpecker is found in a wide range of woodland habitats and gardens, often foraging on small trees. The sound of its pecking is not far carrying.

Bennett's Woodpecker is similar in size to the above two species but appears more robust. It has pale cream underparts lightly speckled with small, round spots, some individuals having only sparse spotting. This woodpecker feeds largely on ants and is often seen on fallen logs or on the ground. Its call is 'whirr-it-whirr-it' or a continuing 'whirritwhirritwhirrit . . .'

The **Red-throated Wryneck** is related to the woodpeckers but it lacks a chisel-like bill and cannot excavate wood, relying instead on the disused nest holes of woodpeckers or barbets. It feeds on ants and termites, which it obtains with its long, sticky tongue. It frequently calls 'kekkekkek' and has a fragmented distribution between the Eastern Cape and Gauteng.

In **Bennett's Woodpecker** (length 22–24 cm) the male's white throat and sides of head are separated by a red moustachial-stripe with black speckling. Females have a brown throat and cheek-patch.

In the **Cardinal Woodpecker** (length 14–16 cm) the male is red and the female black from central crown to nape.

The **Red-throated Wryneck** (length 18 cm), seen here at its nest hole, is told by its brick-red throat and dark, speckled upperparts.

Notes

- Woodpeckers feed mostly on the grubs of wood-borer beetles found within the body of a tree. They probe the beetle burrows with their long, sticky or barbed tongues and find other grubs under the bark.
- Woodpeckers' nest holes are in much demand by other hole-nesting birds that are unable to excavate holes. Starlings, tits, small owls, Grey-headed Sparrows, Wrynecks and many other species are in the queue for a vacated nest hole.

Canaries & siskins

W. Tarboton

The **Yellow-fronted Canary** (length 12 cm) has a horn-coloured bill and mainly yellow body. Both crown and nape are grey.

There are 13 canary species in southern Africa and two of their smaller (at 13 cm) relatives, the siskins. All have dark legs and stoutly conical bills for seed-crushing, and most have attractive songs. Six canaries are yellow and seven are grey-brown, two with yellow rumps. Siskins are small, canary-like birds with dull yellow underparts and brown upperparts. They reveal dull yellow rumps in flight. Both species have very restricted ranges and are found in small flocks only on high mountain slopes.

The most common local canary is probably the **Yellow-fronted Canary**, which until recently was known as the **Yellow-eyed Canary** despite its brown eyes. Its facial pattern is confusingly like that of other yellow canaries, but both nape and crown are grey. It is found in flocks feeding on grass seeds in all types of woodland, bushveld and plantation fringes and has a lively song whch it delivers in short bursts. The sexes are alike.

The dark-billed **Cape Canary** is a less bright yellow than the Yellow-fronted and is told by a broad grey region from nape to hind-neck (but

In the **Yellow Canary** (length 14 cm) the male is yellow – darker in the east as in this KwaZulu-Natal bird seen at a waterhole.

The grey of the hind-neck and nape of the **Cape Canary** (length 13–14 cm), seen here at its nest in a grapevine, does not extend to the crown.

SOME LESS COMMON SOUTHERN AFRICAN CANARIES & SISKINS

Lemon-breasted Canary

Forest Canary

Bully Canary

Black-headed Canary

not crown). Its song is a series of rolling warbles and trills. It is found in small flocks in a variety of habitats from coastal scrub and mountain grassland to protea-covered slopes, mainly in a broad coastal band from the Western Cape to Swaziland and beyond.

The **Yellow Canary** has a broad distribution in the drier western regions, from the Cape northwards. Males and females look very different. Small flocks of these canaries live in low bushes on hillsides and wooded watercourses and in bushveld. They have a vigorous, high-pitched song. Females are white below, streaked black.

Of the grey-brown canaries, the large **Streaky-headed Canary** has the widest southern and inland distribution. Among 'little brown birds', its white eyebrow is shared only by the Yellow-throated Sparrow. It has a pleasant song delivered in short bursts from the top of a tree and is seldom numerous, found singly or in small groups in woodland, fallow farmlands and suburbia. The small **Black-throated Canary** is common and also has a wide distribution. It occurs in small flocks and feeds on grass and weed-seeds in gardens, farmlands and road verges. It sings a sustained and rambling song from the tree tops.

The **Cape Siskin** is restricted to the fynbos-covered coastal hills of the southern Cape. The very similar Drakensberg Siskin is told by its white outer tail feathers and is found only in the scrub and grasslands of the Lesotho mountains. Their ranges do not overlap.

In the **Cape Siskin** (length 13 cm), both male and female are told by white tips to wing- and tail-feathers.

The **Streaky-headed Canary** (length 16 cm) is told by its wide white eyebrow and dark, streaked crown.

Although the diagnostic small black throat-patch is sometimes absent in the grey-brown **Black-throated Canary** (length 12 cm), it can be told by its yellow rump, which is clearly visible in flight.

Black-eared Canary   White-throated Canary   Protea Canary

Notes

• The name 'canary' is derived from the Canary Islands, so named by the Romans around 40 BC because of the numbers of large dogs (*canae*) they found there. The English name Canary Islands became common centuries later, after the Spanish invasion of the islands. The yellow and brown finches on the islands were exported to Europe as singing cage birds and were called 'canaries', probably for lack of an alternative name.

Owls

If disturbed, the **Marsh Owl** (length 36 cm) takes flight and circles overhead, showing its russet wings. It has a distinctly pale facial-disc with dark eyes and small 'ear-tuft' projections on its head.

Humans have been fascinated by owls for centuries and, even today, country people in many parts of the world regard them with fear and superstition, probably because of their strange sounds at night. They are harmless birds that seldom interact with humans and, in fact, help to control rodent pests. Most owls are strictly nocturnal but some are abroad for a few hours in daylight. There are no fewer than 12 owl species, both small and large, in southern Africa.

The brown, medium-sized **Marsh Owl** is often active in the early morning and late afternoon when it may be seen in farmland and moist grassland perched conspicuously on a fence pole or quartering the land in low flight. It roosts and nests on the ground and seldom makes a sound.

One of the most easily seen bushveld owls is the diminutive **Pearl-spotted Owl** which is active during the early and late daylight hours, sometimes as late as 10h00. It has two black spots resembling 'eyes' at the back of its head. This little owl has a far-carrying call – a series of ascending notes – 'tee-tee-tee-tee-tee-tee . . .' – which are followed by a brief pause and a series of descending 'tew-tew-tew-tew-tew . . .' notes.

The **Pearl-spotted Owl** (length 15–18 cm) is small and rotund with well-spotted dark upperparts, pale underparts and piercing yellow eyes – another two seemingly on the back of its head.

SOME LESS COMMON SOUTHERN AFRICAN OWLS

African Wood Owl

African Grass Owl

White-faced Scops Owl

African Barred Owl

Cape Eagle Owl

The most common large nocturnal owl – the one that is seen on roads at night and is frequently blinded and killed by speeding cars – is the **Spotted Eagle Owl**. Despite the exaggerated estimates of its size, it is not our largest owl. It lives in large trees (particularly old eucalypts) or on rocky koppies or on buildings in towns from where its hooting calls can often be heard. It takes advantage of the food to be found in gardens: reptiles, small birds, beetles and scorpions.

Another fairly common town and country owl is the **Barn Owl**, a bird of almost worldwide distribution. Its call is an eerie screech, often heard at night while it quarters the ground in flight. It subsists mainly on rodents and is a boon in farmland. Barn Owls rear many young during outbreaks of rodents, making good use of the food glut while it lasts.

The **Barn Owl** (length 30–33 cm) has dark eyes set in a white, heart-shaped facial-disc but no 'ear-tufts'. Its pale underparts appear almost white at night.

The nocturnal **Spotted Eagle Owl** (length 43–50 cm) has large yellow eyes, distinct 'ear-tufts' and fully feathered legs. A rufous form with orange eyes (right) is less common.

Notes

- The so-called 'ear-tufts' on the heads of some owls are not ears at all but feathers that can be raised or lowered at will. The owl's ears are concealed beneath the feathers at the sides of its facial-disc.
- The Pearl-spotted Owl can often be located by the chattering of small birds clustered around it. This is known as 'mobbing', a form of collective intimidation by several, unrelated birds aimed at discouraging a predator. The predator knows it has lost the advantage of surprise when it is clear that it has been sighted by the potential prey.

Giant Eagle Owl

Pel's Fishing Owl

Parrots & lovebirds

There are five indigenous southern African parrots, one introduced species and, in the north and west, three lovebirds (small highly social parrots). The indigenous parrots occur in forests, mature woodland or bushveld, where they forage in trees and feed on wild fruits, especially those with hard kernels for which their hooked bills are well adapted. Parrots are not seen in urban areas in southern Africa although there is a growing population of the introduced Rose-ringed Parakeet just north of Durban and a small one in Johannesburg, probably the offspring of escaped pets. Flocks of lovebirds frequent semi-arid regions or mature, moist riverine woodland where they feed mostly on the ground.

All species utter shrill shrieks and much experience is needed to know one call from another. Southern African parrots are not as colourful as many South American and Australian species, and have mostly green and brown plumages. Unfortunately, the lovebirds have more brilliant colours and are highly sought by aviarists.

▲
The Brown-headed Parrot (length 23 cm) is a green bird with a brown head, and yellow eyes. Like all parrots, it climbs with the help of its bill, plucking and holding food with its feet.

P. Steyn

▲
Meyer's Parrot (length 23 cm) has a yellow forehead and shoulder-patches, a blue back and dark eyes.

▲
The female of the relatively rare **Rüppell's Parrot** (length 17 cm) has a rich blue belly and back. Both sexes have a yellow 'shoulder'.

SOME LESS COMMON SOUTHERN AFRICAN PARROTS

Rose-ringed Parakeet

Lilian's Lovebird

Black-cheeked Lovebird

Perhaps the most easily seen parrot in the region is the **Brown-headed Parrot**, a fairly common bird of the eastern bushveld, especially in the Kruger National Park. Feeding groups are easily picked up by their far-carrying shrieks. **Meyer's Parrot** is similar in appearance and has a wide northern distribution. The dark brown **Rüppell's Parrot** is restricted to arid woodland in north-west Namibia.

The largest indigenous African species are the endemic **Cape Parrot** and its near-duplicate, the **Grey-headed Parrot**. The Cape Parrot occurs in afromontane forests of the Eastern Cape and southern KwaZulu-Natal where its distribution is highly fragmented. The Grey-headed Parrot is the East African race that extends south through eastern Zimbabwe and into the far northern Kruger. Felling of their nest-trees and illegal capture of birds for the avicultural trade has made both endangered species.

Of the three lovebirds, the **Rosy-faced Lovebird** is the only common species although localized in tree-lined rocky gorges, river courses and dry bush in Namibia. Flocks in flight contrast vividly with their often monotonous and arid surroundings.

▲
The **Grey-headed Parrot** (length 35 cm) is almost a carbon copy of the Cape Parrot, differing only in that it has a grey head and little or no orange on its forehead.

The **Cape Parrot** (length 35 cm) is a bird of evergreen forests with yellowwood trees. Mostly green, it has a buffy-brown head and an orange forehead and shoulder-patches. ▶

G. Lockwood

◀ The **Rosy-faced Lovebird** (length 17 cm) has a red face and throat, apple-green plumage and a blue back.

Notes

- The Cape Parrot prefers to nest in natural or self-excavated holes in mature yellowwood (*Podocarpus*) trees. The felling of numbers of these slow-growing trees has contributed to the bird's low breeding rate and 'Threatened' status. Flocks of parrots often leave the evergreen forests to feed, flying many kilometres to reach known fruiting trees. They return by the same route late in the day to roost.
- Rosy-faced Lovebirds often become so numerous in aviaries that the owners free some birds. They seem able to live successfully in an urban environment.

Orioles

The **Black-headed Oriole** (length 25 cm) is told by its black head and throat and black wing-feathers fringed with white. The male is seen above feeding on an aloe, its forehead smeared in yellow nectar. The sexes are alike.

Orioles are mainly yellow, thrush-sized, pink-billed, insectivorous and frugivorous birds of broad-leaved woodlands with clear, liquid-sounding calls. There are four species in southern Africa. One of them, the elusive Green-headed Oriole, is strictly localized, being confined to the high-altitude evergreen forests found on Mount Gorongosa in central Mozambique.

The **Black-headed Oriole** is a resident species and thus the best known oriole. It is partial to nectar and, in the winter months, its black head is often covered with the yellow pollen of aloe flowers which it probes with a bill that is not well designed for the purpose. This is a common woodland species and appears also in many wooded suburbs, its presence heralded by its liquid 'pheeoo' call. It also has a rasping 'churr' alarm call. The Green-headed Oriole is almost a green copy and even has a similar call.

The **Eurasian Golden Oriole** is a summer non-breeding visitor that frequents the northern broad-leaved woodland regions and, on the coastal fringe, occurs as far south as the Western Cape. Its call, heard more in Europe than in southern Africa, is a ringing 'weela-weeoo'.

The **African Golden Oriole**, the most yellow of the four, is arguably the most striking. It is not common in South Africa and is more likely to be seen in summer in mature riverine woodland north of our boundaries. It makes liquid whistles such as 'wee-er-er-wul' or 'fee-yoo-fee-yoo'.

The entirely yellow **Eurasian Golden Oriole** (length 24 cm) has contrasting black wings and lores (between eye and bill). The female's plumage is duller and greener with some streaking on the breast.

The black eye-stripe of the **African Golden Oriole** (length 24 cm) is present also in juveniles. Females are a more greenish yellow.

Notes

- The Black-headed Oriole may be confused with the smaller Masked Weaver (see pages 36–37), but the oriole is larger and its bill is pink, not black as in the weaver.

Common buntings

The **Golden-breasted Bunting** (length 16 cm) is a colourful bird of stony bush. Its striking head pattern along with chestnut mantle, yellow underparts and orange breast are not easily forgotten.

A bunting is a type of finch. We have five species in southern Africa, three of which are common and identifiable as small, granivorous, ground-feeding birds with conspicuous black-and-white streaked heads that make for easy recognition. The sexes are closely similar. The Lark-like Bunting, although quite common and wide-spread, is one of the dullest-looking birds in our region and is not as easy to identify. Cabanis's Bunting is very uncommon and must be sought in northern Zimbabwe.

The **Cape Bunting** is a near-endemic with a wide distribution. It mostly avoids more arid regions. It prefers rocky, scrub-covered and hilly terrain or coastal sand dunes. Its call is 'cheri-owee' and it has a shrill, canary-like song which it delivers from a rock or tree top.

The **Golden-breasted Bunting** is a very pretty bird found in pairs in open woodland and bushveld, often with stony ground cover. This bunting has a distinct notch in its tail-tip. Its call sounds like 'pret-ty-boyeee', its song 'chip chip chip terrrr' much repeated. Because of its dipping flight action and white outer tail-feathers, it might be confused in flight with a honeyguide (page 127). True identity can be assured only when the bird has settled.

Much at home in rock-strewn bush or scrub and even the bare ground around eroded dongas, **Cinnamon-breasted** (or **Rock**) **Buntings** can be very common locally in rocky, hilly regions, usually in pairs. The call is a brief 'tee-trrr, chirri-chee' repeated at regular intervals.

In the **Cinnamon-breasted Bunting** (length 16 cm) the body and upperparts in both sexes are saturated in a cinnamon colour with blackish feather centres on the upperparts. The bill is black above, dull yellow below.

SOME LESS COMMON SOUTHERN AFRICAN BUNTINGS

Lark-like Bunting

Cabanis's Bunting.

The **Cape Bunting** (length 16 cm) has a grey, sharply tapered seed-eater's bill, chestnut wings and dusky white underparts, and the typical black-and-white bunting head pattern. Local races may be darker or paler.

Cuckoos & coucals

Juv

♂

▲
The **Red-chested Cuckoo** (length 28 cm) is about the size of the Cape Turtle Dove and is easily identified by its brick-red upper breast and well banded underparts.

Cuckoos are well known only by name. They are common and noisy but difficult to see. Brood parasites, they lay their eggs in the nests of entirely unrelated species and take no part in raising their own offspring. Coucals are related to cuckoos but are not brood parasites. They build their own nests and raise their own young.

About a dozen migrant cuckoo species visit southern Africa in summer in search of hosts. Two of them, the Red-chested Cuckoo (better known by its Afrikaans onomatopoeic name Piet-my-vrou) and the Diederik Cuckoo, spend most of the season in and around gardens. Their calls are among the common sounds of summer, yet it is surprising how seldom they are seen or recognized by non-birders.

The **Red-chested Cuckoo** mostly parasitizes robins, the Cape Robin-chat often the chosen garden host for its single egg. It has a rapid hawk-like flight, but remains motionless when it settles, usually high in a tree where it is difficult to detect. It arrives in late September or early October. The male's much repeated call, a loud, ringing 'quid pro quo' (or 'piet-my-vrou'), is

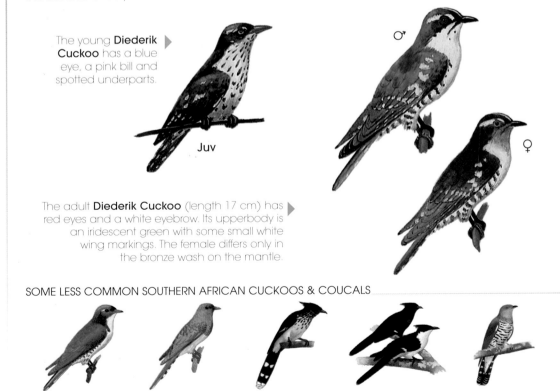

The young **Diederik Cuckoo** has a blue eye, a pink bill and spotted underparts. ▶

Juv

♂

♀

The adult **Diederik Cuckoo** (length 17 cm) has ▶ red eyes and a white eyebrow. Its upperbody is an iridescent green with some small white wing markings. The female differs only in the bronze wash on the mantle.

SOME LESS COMMON SOUTHERN AFRICAN CUCKOOS & COUCALS

Klaas's Cuckoo   Emerald Cuckoo   Striped Cuckoo   Jacobin Cuckoos   European Cuckoo

heard all day and often at night. African, European and Lesser cuckoos have very similar plumage to that of the Red-chested Cuckoo but lack the 'red' chest.

The colourful **Diederik Cuckoo** parasitizes mainly weavers and bishops. Both host species are colonial nesters and attempting to enter one of their nests undetected is a hazardous undertaking for the female cuckoo. A female Diederik being chased all around the neighbourhood by an irate weaver is quite a common sight! As usual among cuckoos, it is the male bird that makes all the noise, its plaintive 'dee dee dee diederik' call heard over and over again throughout the day.

Of the four coucal species of closely similar appearance in southern Africa, only the near crow-sized **Burchell's Coucal** is common. Widespread over much of the eastern regions, it frequents moist vegetation and may visit well-wooded gardens. It is secretive and reveals itself only occasionally although its deep bubbling 'doo doo doo doo . . .' call is often heard descending and ascending the scale about 20 times in succession – like liquid poured again and again from a bottle. This coucal also has a rattling alarm call.

▲ Blind and featherless, the **Red-chested Cuckoo** chick cradles one of its host's eggs between its shoulders, pushing itself against the side of the nest to edge the egg out.

▲ The host's eggs are now on the rim of the nest.

▲ At 12 days the chick is as large or larger than its Cape Robin-chat host, having received abundant food from its busy foster parents.

Juv

▲ **Burchell's Coucal** (length 44 cm) is strikingly coloured with a heavy black bill and ruby-red eyes. A snail-eater and an asset in the garden, it is also a nest-raider that eats other birds' eggs and nestlings.

Great Spotted Cuckoo

Black Cuckoo

Coppery-tailed Coucal

Notes

- When a Diederik Cuckoo lays an egg in its host's nest it normally eats or destroys one of the host's eggs.
- Unlike most birds, cuckoos have a liking for hairy caterpillars. Burchell's Coucal eats a variety of large insects, snails and small reptiles, as well as rodents.

Swifts

Swifts are fast-flying, aerial-feeding birds with a superficial resemblance to swallows (see pages 48–49), which are also specialized aerial feeders. Although distinct groups, both have developed through convergent evolution a streamlined body shape, long and powerful wings, a short wide bill, and short legs. These characteristics and others have evolved for high-speed flight and rapid manoeuvring. Swifts are distinguished from swallows by their dark colouring, long and narrow wings and by their extremely rapid flight.

The tails of swifts may be forked or squarish and their basic colouring is dark brown, many appearing black in flight. Their plumage patterns consist mostly of a small white throat-patch and, possibly, a white patch on the rump or, in a few species, some white on the underparts. Unlike swallows they have no other colour in their plumage. A swift's legs are very short, the feet with sharp claws. Coupled with very long and narrow scimitar-shaped wings, they make it extremely difficult for the bird to take off from the ground without the help of a good breeze.

◄ The **Alpine Swift** (length 22 cm) is told by its white throat and belly and speed of flight.

◄ The **White-rumped Swift** (length 15 cm) has a forked tail and a small white crescent on its rump.

▲
The **Little Swift** (length 14 cm) has a square tail and a large white rump-patch that wraps round the sides of its body.

SOME LESS COMMON SOUTHERN AFRICAN SWIFTS

Bradfield's Swift   Horus Swift   African Palm Swift   Black Swift   Mottled Swift

Swifts cannot perch on a branch or wire as swallows do; but their sharp claws enable them to cling to rough surfaces such as rocks and walls. From this position near their nest or roost they are able to shuffle forward a short distance on their short legs. Becoming airborne again is merely a matter of dropping from a height.

Most frequently seen around towns are the **Little Swift** and the **White-rumped Swift**. These species and the slender, pale brown African Palm Swift, which is never far away from tall palm trees, seem to prefer human habitation. Little and White-rumped swifts often nest under the eaves in buildings and beneath freeway fly-overs. Colonies of Little Swifts nesting under road bridges may fly out as cars pass over. Their white rumps are then conspicuous.

The large **Alpine Swift** makes its home in mountainous regions. It flies so fast that, at close range, its wings make an audible whine. Flocks flying near their roosts in the evening can be heard 'screaming'.

The **Little Swift** collects feathers and grass scraps while in flight and glues them with saliva to make its nest under the eaves.

The scimitar-like wings and short wide bill of an Alpine Swift (right) are clearly seen as it clings to a rock near its nest. Like all swifts, the White-rumped Swift (below) has sharp claws on its feet and can grip rock faces and walls.

Notes

- The most aerial of birds, swifts drink and bathe by splashing into water while flying. They can remain on the wing all night. The European Swift is said to spend about 10 months in Africa between breeding seasons without settling Most swifts, however, return to the nest or a roost at nightfall.
- By flying with their mouths open, swifts and swallows catch a variety of flying insects and small spiders that float on silken webs. A swift with nestlings to feed will forage continuously until its crop is full to bulging. It then returns to its nest and presents the chicks with a substantial ball of insects.
- In prolonged inclement weather adult swifts fly long distances to find food for their nestlings. At this time the nestlings are able to reduce their metabolisms to a state of torpor until the parents return.

Pallid Swift   Mottled Spinetail   Böhm's Spinetail

Waxbills, finches & mannikins

W. Tarboton

The **Blue Waxbill** (length 12–14 cm) is a brilliant blue in the male. Females are a much paler blue.

W. Tarboton

When the **Common Waxbill** (length 13 cm) settles, its red bill, facial-mask and underbelly are striking, the entire underparts washed pinkish and with fine brown barring. Note the dull juvenile in the background.

In the **Melba Finch** (length 12–13 cm) ▶ the male is outstandingly colourful. The female retains the red bill but lacks the red forehead and throat.

These are very small seed-eaters, very colourful but easily overlooked. They are ground-feeders and often feed in mixed groups on open tracks in thornveld, darting off into the bush at the slightest disturbance. With the exception of the Bronze Mannikin, they are seldom found in urban areas. Most species frequent thornveld and all rely on access to water.

The most frequently seen (in game parks) and admired is the **Blue Waxbill**, which is light brown above and powder-blue from face to underparts, the blue paler and more restricted in the female. Small flocks fly into a low thornbush when disturbed on the ground, but soon return to resume feeding. Their call is a high-pitched 'weeet weeet'.

Reedbeds and rank vegetation associated with wetlands and vleis are frequented by flocks of **Common Waxbills**. These little seed-eaters appear to be constantly on the move. As the flock flies off in straggling procession the 'chik chik ZEE' calls confirm the identity of the birds.

Other species feed with blue waxbills, among them the **Melba Finch**. It has a pretty song, but the normal call is a brief 'wick'. Pairs associate with Blue Waxbills but are never as numerous as the waxbills.

SOME LESS COMMON SOUTHERN AFRICAN WAXBILLS, FINCHES & MANNIKINS

Quail Finch | Pink-throated Twinspot | Orange-breasted Waxbill | Black-cheeked Waxbill | Violet-eared Waxbill

Firefinches, small carmine-red birds, are also seen in association with waxbills. The three common species are the **Red-billed Firefinch**, **Blue-billed Firefinch** and **Jameson's Firefinch**, the reddest of the three species. The Blue-billed Firefinch has a rather restricted easterly range and is located by the male's trilling alarm call.

Mannikins are black, white and brown birds with black heads and white underparts. Three species occur, all in the eastern parts of the region. The most common and widespread, the **Bronze Mannikin**, is also the smallest. This tiny, highly social bird is found in flocks in grasslands, old cultivations, bushveld thickets and coastal scrub. It is common in gardens within its range, its call a wheezy 'chik chik chikka'.

The **Bronze Mannikin** (length 9 cm) has bronzy-green wing-spots on its upperparts, a black-and-white bill and barred flanks.

In the **Red-billed Firefinch** ▶ (length 10 cm) the female is mostly a drab grey-brown. The male has a reddish bill.

The **Blue-billed Firefinch** (length 11 cm) is told by its grey-brown crown (absent north of our borders), blue-black bill and black belly.

Jameson's Firefinch (length ▶ 11 cm) has a blue-black bill and black underbelly. The male's carmine colouring permeates its brown upperparts.

Cut-throat Finch

Red-headed Finch

Red-backed Mannikin

Notes

• Blue Waxbills normally build their flimsy grass nest close to a nest of venomous wasps, presumably for protection against intruders. The wasps tolerate the waxbills.

Whydahs, Cuckoo Finch & widow finches

The breeding male **Paradise Whydah** (length 38 cm) is distinguished by its ornate tail-feathers.

A male **Paradise Whydah** (length 12 cm) in transitional plumage, showing white head-stripes like the female's.

Whydahs and widow finches are a totally different family of seed-eaters from widows and, like the Cuckoo Finch, are brood parasites, laying their eggs in the nest of a host species, usually a waxbill. Each species is host-specific. The chicks of both host and parasite grow up together. In the case of the four whydahs, males in breeding plumage can be identified by their elongated tail-feathers twice the length of their bodies.

The **Paradise Whydah** and the **Shaft-tailed Whydah** are found mostly in thornveld, often sparsely distributed, the males instantly recognizable by their tail feathers. In behaviour they are much like the Pin-tailed Whydah. The Melba Finch is host to the Paradise Whydah and the Violet-eared Waxbill to the Shaft-tailed Whydah.

The **Pin-tailed Whydah** is very common, the male easily identified by its summer breeding plumage, red bill and long, fairly stiff tail. The male is polygamous, with up to six mates, and

The young **Cuckoo Finch** (length 12 cm) has a broad-based, short black bill and a rather dumpy appearance. This fledgling is being fed by its foster parent, a Black-chested Prinia.

SOME LESS COMMON SOUTHERN AFRICAN WIDOW FINCHES

Purple Widow Finch

Steel-blue Widow Finch

Green Widow Finch

displays by hovering over feeding females in bouncing flight while twittering continually. Its host is the Common Waxbill.

In the large weaver family, the yellow **Cuckoo Finch (Parasitic Weaver)** is the odd bird out. Fairly nomadic by nature it is commonly overlooked as 'just another weaver'. It is usually found in well-vegetated vleis and mixed grassland with bushes, where it often forms small flocks. The female is a streaky brown bird which resembles the juvenile or a female widow but can be told by its heavy black bill. This little bird parasitizes cisticolas and prinias.

Male widow finches (indigobirds), not least the **Black Widow Finch**, are almost totally black in breeding plumage. They have short tails and are best identified by their combination of bill and leg colours. Female widow finches and whydahs are small and brown-streaked (pale below) and very difficult to identify to species when not with a male. Except for bill colour, non-breeding males resemble females. Widow finches mimic the songs of their hosts (mostly firefinches), the presence of a particular widow finch in summer a clear indication of the host's presence.

In the **Shaft-tailed Whydah** (length 12 cm) the breeding male (length 34 cm) is distinguished by tail-shafts with bulbous tips.

In the **Pin-tailed Whydah** (length 12 cm) the male (length 34 cm) retains its red bill when not in its black-and-white breeding plumage. Females have a dark bill.

In the **Black Widow Finch** (length 11 cm) the male is told by its white bill. All male widow finches often perch conspicuously on telephone wires.

Notes

- Many people know the Pin-tailed Whydah from its visits to the garden, where it and its retinue of females dominate the bird-feeding table. The male immediately chases away all small birds up to the size of a dove.
- Male whydahs are often encountered in partial breeding plumage, either in early summer or in autumn. The beginning of a long tail is the first clue to identity; otherwise, bill colour and the distribution of patches of black in the plumage are a guide.

Rock-jumpers

Two endemic mountain-loving birds, the Cape Rock-jumper and the Orange-breasted Rock-jumper, may be mistaken for rock thrushes (see pages 28–29). Males are told from rock thrushes by the distinctive black-and-white throat and upper breast. Rock-jumpers hop and jump over rocks in a lively manner, raising the tail after landing. Their call is a rapid whistle 'pee-pee-pee-pee . . .'

The Cape Rock-jumper inhabits rocky mountain slopes in the fynbos regions of the south-west Cape whereas the **Orange-breasted** (or **Drakensberg**) **Rock-jumper** is usually found in areas above 2 000 m in KwaZulu-Natal and the adjacent mountains of the Eastern Cape and Lesotho. Both these species are fairly common in their restricted ranges, but there is no overlap in their distribution. Apart from the colour of their underparts, males are closely similar. Females are duller in colour and much less striking.

▲
The male **Cape Rock-jumper** (length 25 cm), shown here on the left, is very similar to the male **Orange-breasted Rock-jumper** (length 21 cm), shown on the right.

Rockrunner

This bird has no connection whatever with the rock-jumpers. It is an aberrant, endemic grass-warbler, a shy, but lively bird of grassy rock- and bush-strewn hillsides and dry watercourses in west-central Namibia. Its song is a fluty, but deep-pitched, mellow warbling of 'trooodle-rooodle' sounds and higher notes, rapidly uttered mostly in the early morning and evening. It can be seen and heard in the Jan Viljoen Game Reserve near Windhoek.

Unlike other grass warblers, the Rockrunner has a heavily streaked head and mantle, distinctive head markings, white throat and breast and rufous rear body. It also has the unusual habit of keeping its tail raised.

▲
With its distinctive tail stance and head and other markings, the **Rockrunner** (length 17 cm) stands out from all other grass warblers.

Common tits

Tits are small insectivorous and arboreal birds with short, stout, black bills. Some are all-black with white wing markings, others have a black head and breast and either white or grey body colours. They forage habitually in woodland tree canopies, often in parties. They have high-pitched, rasping calls.

The near-endemic **Southern Black Tit** is widespread in the eastern and north-eastern regions, often seen feeding in mixed bird parties. Another near-endemic, the **Ashy Tit**, is common in the central regions, but seldom reaches coasts. It is a common bird of thornveld and mixed woodland.

The endemic **Southern Grey Tit** is found in dry thornveld, karoo scrub and rocky gorges in the southern and south-western Cape. As its alternative name implies, the **Northern Grey** (or **Miombo**) **Tit** of Zimbabwe frequents miombo woodland.

In the **Southern Black Tit** (length 16 cm) the male (above) is entirely black except for a white shoulder-patch and white wing-feather edges. The female is greyer, especially on the underbelly.

♀

The **Northern Grey Tit** (length 14 cm) has white underparts and more white on its head than the Ashy Tit.

The **Ashy Tit** ▶ (length 14 cm) has a black-and-white head, throat and upper breast but a pale grey mantle and rear body.

Unlike both Ashy and Southern Black tits, the **Southern Grey Tit** (length 13 cm) has a brown mantle and grey-brown underparts.

SOME LESS COMMON SOUTHERN AFRICAN TITS

Carp's Tit   Rufous-bellied Tit   Cinnamon-breasted Tit

Sugarbirds

There are two endemic South African sugarbirds – not to be confused with sunbirds (see pages 38–39). Sugarbirds are generally brownish in colour with a yellow vent and a long decurved bill.

The distinctive **Cape Sugarbird** is well known for its long tail and its association with protea plants in the southern Cape fynbos biome. They occur within this habitat from the Western Cape to Port Elizabeth. Males and females are very similar, the male with a very long tail. They feed on nectar and small insects found in flowers. So long as proteas are in bloom, the Kirsten-bosch Botanical Gardens in Cape Town are seldom without Cape Sugarbirds.

In **Gurney's Sugarbird** the sexes are also alike, the breast more rufous than in the Cape Sugarbird. Gurney's Sugarbird feeds on proteas, aloes, the exotic bottle-brush and a variety of other flowering plants. It is found on the mountains of the Eastern Escarpment in a broken distribution as far north as Zimbabwe, its quest for flowers in season making it somewhat nomadic.

♂

♀

▲
The tail of the male **Cape Sugarbird** (length 44 cm) is much longer than that of the female (length 30 cm with tail). Males and females frequent proteas in bloom, a female seen below on a flowering *Leucospermum*.
▼

N. Dennis/SIL

▲
In **Gurney's Sugarbird** (length 25–29 cm) the tail is about the same length as the body.

Oxpeckers

There are two oxpecker species in Africa. They are related to starlings but have short legs for clinging to and crawling on the fur of wild ungulates (hooved animals), including cattle. They feed on ticks and blowfly larvae. Both oxpeckers have dark brown upperparts and cream underparts and are easily identified by bill and eye colour. The Yellow-billed has a pale rump.

The **Yellow-billed Oxpecker** prefers to feed on buffaloes, giraffes and rhinoceroses. It is less often tolerated by domestic livestock. Giraffes and cattle as well as certain antelopes tolerate the **Red-billed Oxpecker**. It has a wider distribution than the Yellow-billed Oxpecker in southern Africa and is probably the more common of the two species.

A **Red-billed Oxpecker** (length 20–22 cm) at its nest in a tree hole (above). Its red bill, red eye and conspicuous yellow eye-wattle distinguish it from the **Yellow-billed Oxpecker** (length 22 cm) which has a heavy red-tipped yellow bill and yellow eyes.

Secretarybird

The **Secretarybird** is a large terrestrial bird of prey – a single family, genus and species. The name of the bird is derived from the loose feathers behind the nape, like a secretary's quill (carried behind the ear) in times gone by. Although it flies and soars well, the bird is most commonly seen striding through the veld while foraging for food. At its nest in a thorn tree, it will adopt the 'intruder position', flattening itself with head lowered should it detect the presence of humans.

Basically pale grey with black flight feathers, 'pants' and broad terminal tail-band, the Secretarybird has a greyish hooked bill and its dark eyes are set in a fleshy, orange-coloured facial-patch which flushes red when the bird is excited. It eats rodents, reptiles (including snakes), insects and almost any small terrestrial animal that it can overpower, subduing active prey by stamping on it. Secretarybirds also eat the eggs of ground-nesting birds.

With its extended tail-shafts, a **Secretarybird** can measure 150 cm, with a two-metre wingspan. It has long, pink legs and stands at about 60 cm.

Francolins & guineafowls

G. Lockwood

The francolins and two guineafowl species are among southern Africa's larger gamebirds – a term which has become firmly entrenched for birds that are hunted for food. Broadly speaking, francolins are a type of partridge and the ancestor of the domestic hen. They are best identified to species by familiarity in the field and an ear tuned to their calls.

For those not in regular contact with francolins, identification to species may not be easy. On first sighting (assuming that the bird is not flying), check leg colour. This can be black, red or yellowish. Next check the colour of the beak and whether or not the bird has bare red facial and neck skin. If time permits – and francolins seldom linger – you may notice features of plumage and whether there are spurs on the legs. Try to get as long a look as possible and mentally list features that strike you. Only then refer to the field guide, remembering to check distribution.

Each of the three common francolins has a wide distribution. **Swainson's Francolin** is a highly visible bushveld bird with a harsh call – a far-carrying, crowing 'kraaaaak-kraaaaak-kraaaaak' that fades out gradually. The **Crested Francolin** is

▲ The **Crested Francolin** (length 32 cm) has a black bill and deep-red legs. Its upperparts are reddish-brown streaked white, the underparts buffy and fore-neck heavily spotted black.

Swainson's Francolin (length 34–38 cm) has red ▶ facial and neck skin and black legs. Its bill is black at the tip only. If the bird has red facial and neck skin but red legs, it is the Red-necked Francolin of eastern coastal regions.

SOME LESS COMMON SOUTHERN AFRICAN FRANCOLINS

| Coqui Francolin | Red-billed Francolin | Hartlaub's Francolin | Grey-winged Francolin | Red-necked Francolin | Natal Francolin |

usually found in coveys in bushveld regions. It has a distinct white eyebrow, white under the eye and a white chin, and a characteristic run with tail raised like a bantam chicken. The call is a shrill 'skeer-kinerrik, skeer-kinerrik, skeer-kinerrik', sounding like 'beer and cognac'.

The large **Cape Francolin** occurs in fynbos, wooded kloofs and scrublands. Its call is a high-pitched screeching 'kwe-eek-kwe-eek-kwe-eek-kwe-eeeek-eeeek . . .', rising and then falling in volume and fading at the end. This is the common francolin of the Western Cape.

Although generally thought to be common everywhere, the well-known **Helmeted Guinea-fowl** is in fact scarce or endangered in the Free State and KwaZulu-Natal, mainly because of unsustainable shooting and loss of habitat through sugar cane planting. Its more secretive and wary forest cousin, the blackish **Crested Guineafowl**, is found in low-altitude forest fringes and dense bush and in riverine and coastal dune forests.

Francolins and guineafowls feed on a wide range of foods depending on season and availability. They eat seeds, bulbs, roots, spiders and a variety of insects, including termites.

G. Lockwood

Multiple white feather-edges and white streaking on the underparts impart an overall greyish appearance to the **Cape Francolin** (length 40–45 cm). Its legs are a dull-red, its bill black above and red below.

The blue neck and face, red helmet and horny casque of the **Helmeted Guineafowl** (length 53–58 cm) may be familiar. It is shown here with its chick.

Crested Guineafowls (length 50 cm) get their name from the floppy black feathers on the head. Their head and neck skin is blue-grey with a whitish collar and their eyes are crimson.

| Orange River Francolin | Shelley's Francolin | Red-winged Francolin |

Notes

- Francolins are best viewed from a car, which serves as a mobile hide and permits a much closer approach than when you are on foot. Identifying the birds from their calls can prove very frustrating. The use of a bird-call magnetic tape, obtainable from most wildlife outlets, is recommended.

Bustards & korhaans

W. Tarboton

There are 11 bustard species in southern Africa, five of which are described here. The name 'korhaan' is applied in South Africa only to the smaller species; in other parts of the world, all are called bustards.

Although they forage on foot, bustards are capable of powerful and sustained flight. They have long thick necks, longish stout legs and cryptically coloured plumage that blends well with the surroundings. Birds of open grasslands or savanna, they do not approach human habitation. All are sexually dimorphic, body plumage differing in males and females. Bustards feed on vegetable matter and small vertebrates.

The **Kori Bustard** is the largest of the family and the heaviest flying land bird, second in size only to the Ostrich. Although well distributed, it is nowhere plentiful except in Etosha National Park in Namibia, where several may be seen on any one day. The Kori Bustard quarters the veld with measured strides.

▲ With its huge body, crested head and long yellow legs, the **Kori Bustard** (length 135 cm) is an imposing bird.

◄ With luck, the male **Kori Bustard** may be seen in its remarkable courtship display.

▲ In the **Black-bellied Korhaan** (length 58–65 cm), the male (seen here) is much more conspicuous than the female.

SOME LESS COMMON BUSTARDS AND KORHAANS

White-bellied Korhaan   Blue Korhaan   Rüppell's Korhaan   Karoo Korhaan   Ludwig's Bustard   Stanley's Bustard

Northern and Southern black korhaans are widespread in southern Africa, the latter confined to the southern and south-western Cape. The Northern occurs throughout the Karoo and north towards Johannesburg in the east and Namibia in the west. They are identical on the ground, but in flight the Northern reveals white in the primary feathers which is lacking in the Southern. Females have black bellies and are extremely cryptic whereas males are not only highly visible but are very noisy in the breeding season, their harsh calls of 'kraa-a-a-aak wet-de-wet-de-wet . . .' heard most mornings and all through the day.

The most common bushveld korhaan is the **Red-crested Korhaan**. Its arrow-shaped markings are easily seen from a car when the birds walk in the road, as they frequently do in national parks. Their colouring makes them very difficult to detect in dry grass except in the breeding season when males advertise their territories by flying steeply upwards with much flapping, then suddenly tumbling downwards. The bird also calls from the ground, a loud 'phee phee phee phee . . .'

Another fairly common savanna species is the long-legged **Black-bellied Korhaan**. The female's white belly belies the name! She is extremely well camouflaged.

Only courting male **Red-Crested Korhaans** display a red crest. Males make high display flights in the breeding season and then tumble down abruptly as if shot.

G. Lockwood

A male **Red-crested Korhaan** (length 53 cm) giving its territorial call. In both males and females the upperbody is covered with small, cream, arrow-shaped marks.

The male **Black Korhaan** (length 53 cm) has a black body, head and neck, a large white ear-patch, pink bill and yellow legs. The folded wings and upperbody are tawny, as is the crown.

Notes

- There are no fewer than seven species of bustards in the Western Cape, Karoo and Namibia. Their cryptic plumage blends well with the scrub and dry grasslands of the region so that finding them requires close scrutiny, especially as they tend to 'freeze' when they think they are being watched.

More chats & wheatears

Chats (see also pages 30–31) are easily seen birds of the open veld. Among the drabber chats, those with white rumps are often called wheatears (pronounced 'wheet-e-er'). However, a few wheatears, such as the Capped Wheatear and the male Buff-streaked Chat, have striking plumages and are easily identified. The **Capped Wheatear**, a highly conspicuous bird with a well defined black-and-white head and white underparts, is a resident of short, dry, overgrazed or burnt grasslands. Although similar in size to other chats and wheatears, its distinctive markings and habit of standing erect in open areas cause it to appear much larger. It nests in underground burrows.

The **Mocking Chat** is a lively and very active bird which is seen in pairs on wooded cliffs and rocky hillsides. It raises its tail on settling and can

▲
In the **Mocking Chat** (length 20–23 cm) males have glossy black upperparts and a small white bar on the shoulder or carpal joint. Their burnt-orange underparts and rump are separated from the black breast by a narrow white band.

Head and breast are ▶
purple-grey in the
female **Mocking Chat**

▲
The **Capped Wheatear** (length 18 cm), seen here with food for its nestlings, has a bold white eyebrow and forehead and a white throat extending to its upper breast.

SOME LESS COMMON SOUTHERN AFRICAN CHATS AND WHEATEARS

| Boulder Chat | Arnott's Chat | Northern Wheatear | Sickle-winged Chat |

often be detected by its mellow calls and by its attractive song, which is comprised of imitations of other bird calls.

The endemic **Ant-eating Chat** may be seen perched on an anthill or rock in level or rolling grasslands. It launches itself into hovering flight, revealing pale, almost translucent, flight feathers. This chat has a central distribution, seldom reaching coastal regions and favours dry, even arid grasslands with anthills and antbear burrows, which it may share with the rightful owners. It has a high-pitched, rambling song, but more often utters a sharp 'peek'.

Mountain Wheatears (Chats) occur on mountain or hill slopes with bushes and rocks or anthills, where they perch conspicuously and sing a jumble of fluty notes early or late in the day. They appear also in farmlands.

▲
The **Ant-eating Chat** (length 17 cm) is told by its uniformly dark brown plumage, darkest in the male, which is seen here in typical pose.

The female **Mountain Wheatear** is usually a drab brown with white rump and vent. ▶

▲
The male **Buff-streaked Chat** (length 15–17 cm) is distinctive, the reddish-brown female less so.

Typical plumages of **Mountain Wheatears** (length 17–20 cm). White shoulder-patches, rump and vent and, often, a white cap on grey or black plumage are prominent male features. ▶

Familiar Chat

Karoo Chat

Tractrac Chat

Herero Chat

Longclaws

▲
The orange throat of the **Orange-throated Longclaw** (length 20 cm) is bordered by black. It has entirely yellow underparts and a broad yellow eyebrow, its upperparts grey-brown.

Longclaws are actually colourful pipits, so named for their very long hind-claws. There are three species, their underparts so distinctly coloured as to make positive identification simple.

The **Orange-throated Longclaw** is a fairly common endemic resident of the eastern and southern parts of South Africa, with an isolated population in Zimbabwe. This is a bird of lush grassveld where it is clearly visible from time to time standing erect on a tuft of grass. It has a 'mewing' call and far-reaching whistle and often calls when flying. Its white tail-tip is prominent in flight.

The **Yellow-throated Longclaw** inhabits moist, lightly wooded grasslands or open woodland in the eastern parts of southern Africa. It sings from the top of a bush 'trioo trioo, troo chit troo . . .' and also makes a monotonous mewing.

The attractive **Pink-throated Longclaw** prefers marshy grassland and the fringes of pans, where it lies low when approached or makes off in erratic flight, revealing its dark upperparts and white wing-bars. It occurs sparsely in coastal KwaZulu-Natal, the Harare area of Zimbabwe and the Okavango Delta in northern Botswana. In the breeding season (summer) the male sings loudly from a bush perch.

▲
The black gorget of the **Pink-throated Longclaw** (length 20 cm) separates its deep rose-red throat and underparts in full breeding plumage. Upperparts are blackish-brown, the feathers edged tawny.

▲
The **Yellow-throated Longclaw** (length 20 cm) has entirely yellow underparts and a yellow eyebrow. The throat is separated by a bold black gorget that expands from the base of the bill. Its upperparts are brown, with all feathers edged yellow

Notes

• The Yellow-throated Longclaw may be confused with the Bokmakierie shrike (see page 86) which has a similar colouring but a heavier bill, a grey nape and a green back, unlike the Yellow-throated Longclaw's brown upperparts.

Dikkops

There are two dikkop species in southern Africa, both noisy nocturnal birds. Although fairly common in suitable habitats, both are cryptically coloured and easily overlooked. Both have the same bill, eye and leg colours and large yellow eyes (indicative of a nocturnal lifestyle).

The **Spotted Dikkop** is a fairly large plover-like bird found in rocky grasslands (often with scattered trees), open ground in woodland and in large gardens. During the day it roosts under a bush or among rocks. It becomes active only after sunset, and its shrill, eerie 'chwee-chwee, chwee-chwee, chwee chwee, tiu tiu tiu . . .' call, trailing off towards the end, can be heard at this time and through much of the night. It is especially active on moonlit nights. If disturbed at the roost it will run off with lowered head and fly reluctantly.

The **Water Dikkop** is the smaller of the two dikkops, usually found on the banks of large rivers or dams. Its call, heard soon after sunset, is a melancholy, piping 'whee, wheeoo-wheeoo . . .' trailing off and starting again. It lies-up during the day in waterside herbage but can be very noisy at night. It is often found on roads near rivers when the moon is bright.

The **Water Dikkop** (length 40 cm) has a wide grey bar surmounted by smaller black-and-white bars on each wing. It has a black moustachial-streak.

Except for a white underbelly, the **Spotted Dikkop** (length 44 cm) is khaki-brown with very dark brown all-over mottling. It is seen here at its nest with two large eggs.

Notes

- The name 'dikkop' is a purely southern African name. For some mysterious reason they are called 'thick-knees' in other parts of the world although their tibio-tarsal joint is no thicker than that of the larger plovers. In Britain, dikkops have always been called 'stone-curlews' although curlews belong to a quite different family.
- Like plovers, dikkops nest on the ground in a shallow scrape. They are normally crepuscular and nocturnal, but on heavily overcast days they may become active and start calling in the daytime.

Gulls & terns

▲
The **Cape Gull** (length 60 cm) has black upper-parts, white head and underparts, a bright yellow bill with a red spot beneath the tip, and dark eyes.

▲
Hartlaub's Gull (length 38 cm) has an entirely white head when it is not in breeding plumage. At this time its bill and legs are a dull red.

A grey head, red bill and legs, and ▶ pale yellow eyes are diagnostic of the **Grey-headed Gull** (length 42 cm).

Although confusingly similar, gulls and terns differ in appearance and behaviour. Both have webbed feet, but gulls have an erect stance and walk easily on proportionately long legs. Terns have a horizontal stance on disproportionately short legs, preferring to fly rather than walk.

Whereas gulls have fairly short, robust bills, terns have longish, slender bills, in many cases approaching the length of the head. Gulls have tails that are rounded or have only a shallow fork. Sea terns, especially, have well-forked tails, often with tail-streamers. Those that frequent inland waters (known as 'marsh terns') tend to have more square tails. The sexes are alike in all gulls and terns and all can swim.

Three gull species are commonly seen in southern Africa. The **Cape Gull** (formerly the Kelp Gull) is the largest and most conspicuous, adults as well as brownish immature birds wide-spread on our coastline. The **Grey-headed Gull** is adapted both to inland and coastal waters. The great lakes of sub-Saharan Africa support large numbers of the species, the most common gull along the KwaZulu-Natal coast. A major breeding

SOME LESS COMMON SOUTHERN AFRICAN TERNS

Little Tern   Lesser Crested Tern   Damara Tern   Arctic Tern   Antarctic Tern

colony exists at a bird sanctuary in Benoni, near Johannesburg. **Hartlaub's Gull** is found mostly on the south-western Cape and Namibian coasts. It seldom ventures inland.

Southern African gulls are basically coastal scavengers that feed on dead seafood and scraps at the shoreline and on discarded offal from fishing boats in harbours (and, in the case of the Grey-headed Gull, at inland rubbish dumps). They seldom eat live fish, unlike those gull species that live and feed mostly in the ocean, especially the Atlantic Ocean.

Terns, for the most part, are elegant seabirds that follow fish shoals and make aerial dives to catch them. They usually forage in flocks that come to rest on shorelines and in estuaries. Among our more common terns are the large **Caspian Tern**, which occurs both on large inland waters and at coastal estuaries, and the slightly smaller **Swift Tern**, another sea tern common in small groups at coastal waters.

Master these two terns and three gulls with the aid of your fieldguide, and you will feel more confident when tackling others in the family. Remember that when terns are not breeding, the front of the head is white. Terns are a difficult group to come to grips with, especially for inland-based birders, and, initially, are best identified at rest when their bill and leg colours can be seen. Their identity in flight is best left until later.

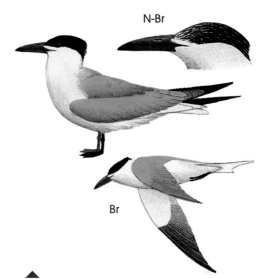

N-Br

Br

▲
The **Caspian Tern** (length 52 cm) has a conspicuous red bill and, when in breeding condition, a full black cap.

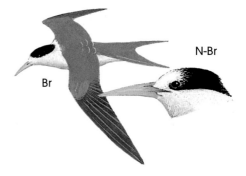

N-Br

Br

The **Swift Tern** (length 50 cm) has a yellow bill and ▶ (like most terns) a black cap when breeding. At other times, it has a partial black cap and white forehead. ▼

P. Steyn

Roseate Tern   Sandwich Tern   Common Tern

Notes

- Terns make only shallow dives when feeding and usually fly off again immediately. Many terns, especially those of inland waters, merely pluck spiders and insects from the surface without deviating from their flight path.
- Sea terns, for example the Arctic Tern, often migrate over long distances. The Arctic Tern, which migrates south after breeding in far northern latitudes, is a common visitor to South African and South American coasts in the southern summer. It has also been recorded in Australian waters – for some individuals a round trip of 35 000 km.
- Since so many gull species seldom or never venture far from the coast they are more accurately called 'gull' rather than by the outdated term 'seagull'.

Pelicans, Gannet & Oystercatcher

Of the seven pelican species in the world, two occur in southern Africa. As its name suggests, the **Great White Pelican** (also called the **Eastern White Pelican**) is the larger. It is nowhere common and is most frequently seen on the coast between Cape Town and northern Namibia, in the Okavango Delta in northern Botswana and at Lake St Lucia in Maputoland. The **Pink-backed Pelican** is less widespread, the greatest reporting rates being from the Okavango Delta and Lake St Lucia region, with scattered sightings between. The pink back feathers are not a field feature.

There are three gannet species in the world: European, Australian and southern African. The **Cape Gannet** is a medium to large, white shore-based seabird, which is endemic to southern African coastlines. Gannets are the temperate-water counterparts of the boobies of tropical

▲
The **Pink-backed Pelican** (length 135 cm) has more greyish plumage than the Great White. In flight, the birds show grey underwings, darkest on the flight feathers. They nest in colonies in trees.
▼

▲
◄ The **Great White Pelican** (length 180 cm) is a basically all-white bird which reveals black wing-feathers in flight. The bill appears even larger when the bird is at rest.

N. Myburgh

waters. They are fish-eating birds that plunge into the sea for their prey from a height. In June, gannets follow migrating sardine shoals northwards along the Natal coast and can be seen from shore in a feeding frenzy as they plunge, repeatedly, to catch the fish.

The endemic **African Black Oystercatcher** – the only oystercatcher species likely to be seen locally – feeds on rocky shores, mainly on the Cape and Namibian coastlines. It also occurs on the east coast, singly or in small groups, and in estuaries as far as the Eastern Cape. African Black Oystercatchers can be difficult to detect amid the black rocks in the inter-tidal zone where they mostly feed. They are most easily spotted when feeding in the sandy estuaries to which they often retreat at high tide and in rough seas. At high water, they tend to join flocks of resting gulls on sandbanks.

The Oystercatcher nests at the high-tide mark on sandy beaches, placing its eggs among blackish dried kelp where the incubating bird is well concealed. If disturbed, it leaves its eggs or small chicks unattended, causing them to die from exposure. Breeding success has diminished in recent years as a result of disturbance on the beaches, especially by 4x4 vehicles.

▲

In response to changing water levels and the availability of food, **Great White Pelicans** may appear unexpectedly at inland waters.

▲

The **Cape Gannet** (length 84–94 cm) has a yellow head and hind-neck, black tail and flight feathers and intricate head markings. It roosts and breeds on offshore islands in colonies that may reach several thousand.

▼

▲

The **African Black Oystercatcher** (length 50 cm) is jet black with a longish red bill, red eye-ring and red legs.

Notes

- The best place to see a large assembly of Cape Gannets breeding is from a viewing hide at Lambert's Bay in the Western Cape in September and October.
- In spite of their large size and awkward gait on land, pelicans are extremely capable and elegant flying birds, soaring on outstretched wings to great heights on warm days.

Difficult to identify

Cisticolas and other warblers

Generally speaking, warblers are small-to-tiny insectivorous birds with slender bills and unobtrusive plumage colours. This miscellaneous group includes cisticolas and other grass warblers, reed warblers, apalises, crombeks, tit-babblers, eremomelas, prinias and others. Several small birds that can easily be identified by colouring, shape or behaviour are also members of this somewhat arbitrary grouping.

Rattling Cisticola

As you will see in your fieldguide, cisticolas (pronounced 'sis-tik-o-la') have very similar plumage colours. It takes perseverance and study over several breeding seasons to really become acquainted with cisticolas. To recognize individual species, a birder must be familiar with specific habitat requirements, flight displays when breeding and calls – three aspects that are observable simultaneously only in summer. To complicate things further, many cisticolas perform their display antics at a great height, often out of sight. Having a copy at hand of *LBJs made easier* (see references, page 133) will help you to meet the challenge of warbler identification.

Palearctic warblers

Millions of Palearctic warblers breed in Europe and migrate south annually to Africa every year in the southern summer. The very word 'Palearctic' quite unnecessarily strikes fear into many hearts. It is merely the name given to the zoogeographical region from North Africa northwards to (and including) Europe and Asia. Africa south of the Sahara is known as the Afrotropical region.

Palearctic warblers are for the most part very plain, brownish birds. Many, but not all, frequent wetland reeds and similar waterside growth. Although distinct from local (Afrotropical) warblers, their general colouring may be very similar to that of some local warblers of the same habitat. They are mostly secretive, but some have recognizable songs. The Willow Warbler is of particular interest as it becomes a common garden bird in summer in southern Africa, except in the arid far west of the region.

Willow Warbler

Nightjars

Nightjars are soft-plumaged, insect-hunting birds with a short bill and wide gape surrounded by stiff bristles. They have large eyes and short, weak legs. Assuming that the name originates in Britain, 'nightjar' probably refers to the 'jarring' sound of the local species' call. In America nightjars are called 'goat-suckers' or 'nighthawks'.

Fiery-necked Nightjar

Nightjars are entirely nocturnal in their habits, hunting flying insects by night and lying-up on the ground or in a tree during the day. Their colouring is so cryptic that they can be almost trodden on before they flush. Since they are active only in the dark they are best identified by their calls or by in-hand inspection of wing and tail patterns (perhaps from road kills as nightjars habitually settle on country roads at night and are often killed by cars).

Larks

Larks are small (length 12–18 cm), resident, terrestrial, brown birds. The spectrum has many tones and shades of brown and the plumages of larks certainly make use of them all, often within the same species. Bill shape is also very variable. Larks have clear calls and a number of different flight displays, but are initially a difficult group to become acquainted with.

Melodious Lark

Pipits

Many birders tend to group pipits and larks together as one large, confusing family of brown terrestrial birds best left for another day's study. Larks, however, are a walkover compared with pipits, many of which are so similar that differentiation in the field is almost impossible in the absence of certain clues or in poor light. When you begin to feel brave enough to struggle with pipit identification, you will be in the company of many experienced birders. Meanwhile, there are three colourful pipits called longclaws (see page 120) that are easier to identify.

Grassveld Pipit

Sandgrouse

Southern Africa has four species of sandgrouse (length 25–30 cm) – pigeon-like birds with marked sexual dimorphism, which are seen either in pairs or in large flocks when they come to water. Three species live in very arid conditions in the western parts of the region and normally avoid contact with humans. They fly fast and are able to cover long distances. The fourth, the Double-banded Sandgrouse, so named for the black-and-white bands on the male's forehead and across its lower breast, is found in the lowveld, often in the Kruger National Park. Pairs are sometimes flushed from the roadside, especially in the northern part of the park. Cryptically coloured, they are easily overlooked and generally difficult to observe, especially as they tend to turn their backs to the observer in readiness for a rapid takeoff.

Double-banded Sandgrouse

Honeyguides and honeybirds

Honeyguides are brood parasites (like cuckoos and whydahs) – they lay their eggs in the nests of other birds, in many cases hole-nesting woodpeckers and barbets. The birds feed on bee grubs and beeswax and are named for the unique habit of certain species of leading humans to bees' nests. Although lost in most areas today, this habit of 'leading' continues where hunter-gatherers are still active as in the Okavango Delta. When the hunters break open bees' nests to get the honey the honeyguides get their reward. Members of the family that do not guide are now called honeybirds.

Lesser Honeyguide

Honeyguides generally have very dull plumage and are easily overlooked unless they show their white outer tail-feathers in flight or make their diagnostic calls. The two most often seen, the Greater Honeyguide and Lesser Honeyguide, are active guiders. The third active guider is the Scaly-throated Honeyguide.

Coursers

Coursers superficially resemble the larger plovers (see pages 66–67) but are much smaller (length 20–28 cm). They generally lack a hind toe. Several species inhabit open terrain, either in small groups or in pairs, and are at least partially nocturnal. They run swiftly on long, spindly legs, some with exaggerated head jerks or rear body-bobbing movements. They are mostly sparsely distributed and many are nomadic, infrequently encountered and not easily seen. There are five species of coursers in southern Africa.

Burchell's Courser

Pratincoles

Pratincoles are related to coursers, but are quite different in appearance. Two of the three southern African species are closely similar summer visitors; the third is a resident found on mid-stream rocks of the Zambezi river system. Pratincoles have short legs and elongated body shapes. They feed in the air, usually in flocks, like large swallows in elegant flight.

Red-winged Pratincole

BIRDS OF PREY

Diurnal (i.e. day-hunting) birds of prey, or raptors as they are called, are very attractive birds but are difficult to identify accurately, the exception being the easily recognized ground-hunting Secretarybird (see page 113). Owls – the only nocturnal birds of prey – are relatively easy to identify (see pages 96–97).

Not only are there several different groups of raptors with various hunting behaviours, but young birds mostly have very different plumages from those of adults and, especially in some of the larger eagles, may take several years to reach maturity. The well-known African Fish Eagle is a good example. If you have not actually seen one of these birds, you will probably recognize it and its far-carrying call from films, videos and magazine articles. The juvenile Fish Eagle in its first plumage looks quite different. It will be about five years before this young bird begins to look like its parents. As a matter of interest, adult female raptors are invariably larger and more powerful than males.

All raptors, except the Secretarybird, are either aerial hunters or scavengers, **vultures** being the best known among the latter. Vultures share a number of features with eagles, such as broad wings with the primary feathers held spread like the fingers of a hand, and are difficult to identify, especially when flying. They are Africa's cleansing team, helping to dispose of carrion, and are not equipped to kill as they lack grasping talons.

At the remains of other animals' kills, a large number of vultures of different species may be seen squabbling and vying actively for prime position. White-backed Vultures (length 90–98 cm) are likely to be in the majority, many of them immatures without the white back. Always dominating at such a feast is the Lappet-faced Vulture (length 115 cm), a mostly black bird with bare, red facial skin. The smallest of the group is likely to be the Hooded Vulture (length 70 cm), best told by its slender bill. Be aware that certain eagles scavenge and that immature Bateleur and Tawny eagles will attempt to snatch their share once the feeding frenzy has abated. A non-raptor, the huge Marabou Stork (see page 71), may also arrive at a kill, towering over the vultures as it pecks and picks at leisure.

On such occasions one can appreciate the large size of most vultures in comparison with the **eagles** that are present. Like vultures,

White-backed Vulture

eagles spend much time foraging on the wing. There are 12 southern African eagles. Most are resident and several species are quite small (about 46 cm as opposed to 80–90 cm, the length of larger ones). Martial, Black and Crowned eagles are the most powerful eagles. The Martial Eagle hunts over bush and woodland, the Black Eagle over mountains and rocky gorges and the Crowned Eagle in forests. Regardless of size, true eagles are told by their fully feathered legs. Only their feet are unfeathered. All other birds of prey, including the Fish Eagle, Bateleur Eagle and the snake eagles, have unfeathered lower legs.

Martial Eagle

Buzzards (watch for the bare legs!) are often mistaken for eagles because of their general shape and large size. They may in fact be larger than some small eagles. For example, the migrant Honey Buzzard (length 60 cm) is larger than Ayres' Hawk Eagle, which reaches a maximum length of 55 cm. Buzzards frequently indulge in soaring flight, using warm rising air columns to keep aloft, as do vultures and eagles, but their flights are usually of short duration. The rest of a buzzard's day is

Jackal Buzzard

spent on a perch from where it still-hunts. Buzzards tend to prey on rodents, reptiles and small birds, the exception being the Honey Buzzard which favours bee and wasp grubs. A common buzzard of hilly regions is the resident Jackal Buzzard (length 44–53 cm), which often perches on roadside telephone poles. Unlike many other buzzards, it is strikingly marked.

Yellow-billed Kite

Two very similar large, migrant **kites** are with us in the southern summer: the common Yellow-billed Kite and the less common Black Kite. Both are fork-tailed brown raptors measuring 55 cm in length. The Yellow-billed Kite is a partial scavenger, often foraging on highways in search of small animals killed by traffic. It flies low and is easily seen. A third, smaller, bird is the resident Black-shouldered Kite (length 30 cm), a grey-and-white raptor with black shoulder-patches that can be seen hovering over roads on the lookout for small rodents.

Ovambo Sparrowhawk

Goshawks and **sparrowhawks** (length 23–60 cm) are basically the same although goshawks tend to be larger. These mostly greyish hawks are characterized by sleek bodies, long slender legs and longish tails and by dashing flights of brief duration. They catch flying birds in swift aerial pursuit from the cover of a leafy tree and are secretive when not hunting. The Pale Chanting Goshawk is less secretive and hunts from an exposed perch. **Harriers** (length 44–56 cm) are long-winged, long-tailed and long-legged hawks that inhabit grasslands or marshes. They fly low, in a leisurely manner, as they quarter the ground for prey. Harriers settle on the ground or perch on a post, seldom in a tree.

Bat Hawk

There are four monospecific **hawks**, i.e. hawks with only one species in the genus or family. The Bat Hawk is a sparsely distributed resident bird of wooded regions which feeds mainly on bats that it catches in flight at night or at dusk. It roosts during the day. The Osprey, a fish-eating hawk, is an uncommon summer visitor which is found on large inland waters and coastal lagoons. It hunts mostly from a perch and catches fish in a shallow dive. A third species, the Gymnogene (African Harrier Hawk), is a fairly common resident in a variety of wooded habitats. Adults are mainly grey with bare, yellow skin on their faces; young birds have brown plumage. This hawk hunts by exploring cavities in trees or in rocks or searches the nests of other birds for nestlings, lizards and other small creatures. Lastly, there is the African Cuckoohawk, a raptor of woodlands and forest fringes. It is widely known as one of the 'bazas', of which there are five species world-wide. Adults have crested heads and cuckoo-like well-barred underparts; immatures have spotted underparts. This sluggish bird has a leisurely flight and feeds largely on lizards.

Black Harrier

Peregrine Falcon

Falcons and their smaller relatives, **kestrels,** are birds of very rapid flight when hunting. They bring down other birds by diving from above or overtake prey in level flight. Kestrels are the more gentle in their hunting methods and mostly take small birds, rodents or, in many species, flying insects such as grasshoppers. Several kestrels are able to hover for long periods when foraging over grasslands.

Quails

True quails (length 15–18 cm) are diminutive francolins, but are solitary, nomadic and irruptive by nature; francolins are generally gregarious and mostly sedentary. Hartlaub's Francolin (length 25–30 cm) is the smallest francolin. Quails are normally seen in pairs or family groups, usually as they flush at one's feet. Three species occur in southern Africa: the Blue Quail, a rare summer visitor, found mostly in Zimbabwe and Mozambique; the Harlequin Quail, a summer resident; and the Common Quail, which is both a resident and a visitor. It is highly nomadic and erratic and its presence in any region is uncertain from year to year.

Blue Quail

Button quails

In spite of the name, button quails (length 14–15 cm) are quite unrelated to true quails. There are three species in southern Africa, belonging to a group of birds known as hemipodes. Button quails have subdued plumage colours, russet-brown above and white below. They tend to be very secretive in grassveld where, like true quails, they are seen only when flushed. Unless surprised, however, they are reluctant to flush. Their presence in the veld may be detected by their 'wit wit wit' calls.

Hottentot
Button Quail

Snipes

There are two true snipes in southern Africa, the resident African Snipe (length 32 cm), previously called the Ethiopian Snipe, and the Great Snipe (length 35 cm), which is a rare summer visitor. The snipe that you are likely to see in marshlands, swamps and inundated grasslands is the African Snipe. It has a very long, rapier-like bill, short legs and tail, and well-barred and -striped head and body. It will flush ahead of you when you are walking, making off at a low level with a soft 'chuck' and following a zig-zag pattern of flight before resettling. It may also be seen in very shallow inland waters where it wades while probing the mud. If you have access to a bird sanctuary and can spend an hour or so concealed in the hide near water, you are sure to see the African Snipe.

African Snipe

Shorebirds

Shorebirds is a term for a number of small to medium-sized, mainly greyish, water-associated species that visit Africa as non-breeding visitors, feeding on the shorelines of coasts, lagoons, estuaries and inland waters. The American term 'shorebird' is used here since it is more descriptive and less confusing than the alternative name 'wader', which covers the many birds that walk and feed in water.

Little Stint

Shorebirds breed in the far northern regions of Europe, Scandinavia and Siberia during the northern summer, at which time many adopt more colourful plumages. They migrate south into Africa in enormous numbers during the southern spring wearing their dull, non-breeding colours. Shorebirds are superficially similar to small plovers and are an intriguing but very difficult group of birds for even experienced birders to get to grips with.

Some shorebirds, in particular the Sanderling and White-fronted Sandplover, are easily seen when on the beach. Both follow a receding wave while probing the wet sand and then – just as the next wave sweeps in – turn and run in front of it at high speed.

Black-browed
Albatross

Southern ocean birds

These totally marine birds are mostly wide-ranging ocean wanderers, among them the various petrels, shearwaters, fulmars and prions. They are unwilling visitors to continental shores, preferring to breed on ocean islands, and vary in size from the great albatrosses to the diminutive storm petrels. They have dark upperparts and whitish underparts with few distinctive identifying features except bill colour.

To see ocean birds it is necessary to go to sea. Many ardent birders do so on fishing trawlers. Even so, large numbers of birds come close to the boats only in rough and windy weather when ocean swells make viewing difficult. Ocean birds are a great attraction for birders with good sea legs and strong constitutions. 'Starters' are advised, however, to delay their first ocean foray for a while.

Difficult to find

Some birds are quite easy to identify – once you have found them. The distinctive **Narina Trogon** (length 29–34 cm) is one such species, a handsome bird with scarlet underparts and glossy green upperparts; females are only a little duller. Even in your early days of birding you will probably hear the name of this bird bandied about by those who boast of having spotted it and those who regret that they have not. Where they do occur, Trogons are not that difficult to find and, with a little stealth and patience, you may well see one, especially if you can locate the call – a low, unhurried 'hooot hoot, hooot hoot . . .' made as if through closed lips. A bird of the evergreen forests of the eastern regions, the Trogon is heard mostly in early summer during its breeding season. Birds in the higher forests tend to move eastwards to lower altitudes during the colder months.

Narina
Trogon

Your first sight of a Narina Trogon will probably be of its back. It will slowly turn its head and – if you are still and quiet – it may even turn around and display its crimson underparts. (Or it may fly off!) It is insectivorous and frugivorous, and nests in a tree-hole.

The **African Pitta** (length 23 cm) is another highly coloured enigmatic bird. Finding it usually means a lengthy journey to the Zambezi Valley in mid-summer. The birds migrate to southern Africa from East Africa to breed in November (when the summer rains are at their heaviest) and disappear again in February. Most Pittas do not go further south than the Zambezi Valley.

African Pitta

To find the Pitta it is advisable to join a group with a guide who knows where to look and what to look for. The bird favours dense thickets in riverine forests and the search for it may involve some backache and much crawling on hands and knees. The Pitta does not have a far-ranging call; it makes a rather subdued 'burp' during brief flutters from the ground. Finding it requires determination, but is well worth the effort.

Painted
Snipe

The **Painted Snipe** (length 28–30 cm) – a colourful and very uncommon bird – is not in any way related to the true snipes. The female (shown here) is more colourful than the male, olive brown on the upperparts and head, white below, with a bold white band encircling the folded wing, and a white eye-stripe and central stripe on the crown. The male has a grey head and neck and heavily barred wings, but otherwise the same arrangement of white markings as the female. The birds are usually seen in pairs on the muddy shores of small ponds with dense vegetation at the fringes. They are shy and retiring and disappear into the vegetation at the slightest disturbance, but they seldom flush and will tolerate the approach of a slow-moving vehicle.

African Finfoot

The **African Finfoot** (length 63 cm) is neither duck nor cormorant but, in appearance, somewhere between the two. Males and females are similar, both with diagnostic red bills and feet. They occur on quiet rivers with overhanging trees and bushes, mostly in the eastern and north-eastern regions, swimming close to the banks beneath branches. Although they are secretive and undemonstrative, a quiet wait on the riverbank is often rewarded with a sighting.

A rare summer visitor to coastal KwaZulu-Natal is the **Crab Plover** (length 38 cm), a mostly white bird with a black back and flight feathers, robust black bill, and long blue-grey legs. (Single birds have also been sighted on a few occasions in the Eastern Cape.) Because of its striking pied plumage and heavy black bill, the bird is unlikely to go unnoticed. It breeds in the Persian Gulf and is usually seen in small flocks on sandy seashores, estuaries and mangrove flats on remote islands off the East African and Mozambican coasts. The Crab Plover is not easily approached and flocks flush readily, uttering a harsh 'kra-ka' in flight.

Crab Plover

The **African Broadbill** (length 14 cm) is a an uncommon and elusive resident in lowland and coastal forests. It has a wide bill, dumpy appearance and well-streaked, white underparts, the male with a black cap. The bird is often difficult to locate and may be absent from apparently ideal habitats. It makes a display flight in the horizontal plane while puffing its white rump feathers and calling a frog-like 'purr-rupp'. At other times it may be seen hawking insects like a flycatcher.

African Broadbill

The **Spotted Creeper** (length 15 cm) is a secretive and uncommon localized resident which is found mostly in miombo woodland in Zimbabwe and Mozambique. It has a long, down-curved bill and clambers about tree trunks like a wood-pecker, calling a series of rapid, sibilant notes 'sweepy-swip-swip-swip . . .'

Spotted Creeper

Of southern Africa's three resident mannikins (see pages 106–107), the relatively large **Pied Mannikin** (length 12–13 cm) is by far the most scarce. It occurs in coastal bush, dune forests and bamboo thickets along the eastern KwaZulu-Natal coast and, more widely, in Mozambique and eastern Zimbabwe. This striking bird has a black head, heavy conical bill and bold black flank markings. Its call is a chirruping 'pee-oo'.

Pied Mannikin

The endemic **Neergaard's Sunbird** (length 10 cm) occurs in a narrow band along the northern KwaZulu-Natal and Mozambique coasts in mixed dry woodland and dune forests. The male's small size, short bill, blue rump and grey (not black) underparts distinguish it from similar sunbirds. Pairs forage inconspicuously in the canopy at the fringes of forests and can sometimes be located by the male's sharp descending 'chee-ti-ti' call. Another

**Neergaard's
Sunbird**

bird of the eastern parts of the region, the evasive and secretive **Yellow-spotted Nicator** (length 23 cm), occurs in dense bush and riverine forests from KwaZulu-Natal northwards. The bird has also been sighted in the eastern part of Kruger National Park and in the Zambezi river valley. A relative of the bulbuls, it is identified by green upperparts, bold yellow spots on the folded wing, buffy to white underparts, a yellow vent and a heavy shrike-like bill. The sexes are alike. The call is a rich jumble of mellow trills and warbles.

**Yellow-spotted
Nicator**

Two birds best sought in the the Vumba region in eastern Zimbabwe, just south of Mutare, are **Swynnerton's Robin** (length 14 cm) and the Silvery-cheeked Hornbill. Like most difficult-to-find birds, Swynnerton's Robin is not uncommon in its preferred montane evergreen forest habitat and, while looking for it, you are likely to discover many other lessseen species in the forests and their fringes. (A night spent in the vicinity of the 'Seldom Seen Lodge' or the nearby 'Leopard's Rock Hotel' should prove rewarding.) The huge **Silvery-cheeked Hornbill** (length 75–80 cm) has a massive pale bill and casque (smaller in the female). Listen for the braying call of these hornbills; they are usually found in pairs in fruiting trees.

**Swynnerton's
Robin**

**Silvery-cheeked
Hornbill**

REFERENCES

BARNES, KN (ed). 2000. *The Eskom Red Data Book of Birds of South Africa, Lesotho and Swaziland.* BirdLife South Africa, Johannesburg.

CAMPBELL, B & LACK, E (eds). 1985. *A Dictionary of Birds.* Calton (Poyser) and Vermillion (Buteo).

HARRISON, JA, ALLAN, DG, UNDERHILL, LG, HERREMANS, M, TREE, AJ, PARKER, V & BROWN, CJ (eds). 1997. *The Atlas of Southern African Birds*, vols 1 & 2. BirdLife South Africa, Johannesburg.

FRY, CH. 1984. *The Bee-eaters.* Russel Friedman Book Enterprises, South Africa.

LITTLE, R, CROWE, T & BARLOW, S. 2000. *Gamebirds of Southern Africa.* Struik Publishers, Cape Town.

MACLEAN, GL (ed). 1993. *Roberts' Birds of Southern Africa.* John Voelcker Bird Book Fund, Cape Town.

NEWMAN, KB (ed). 1971. *Birdlife in Southern Africa.* Purnell & Sons, Johannesburg.

NEWMAN, KB, *et al.* 2000. *Birds by Colour.* Struik Publishers, Cape Town.

NEWMAN, KB. 2002. *Newman's Birds of Southern Africa.* Struik Publishers, Cape Town.

NEWMAN, KB, SOLOMON, D, JOHNSON, D & MASTERSON, A. 1998. *LBJs Made Easier.* Southern Books, Johannesburg.

INDEX OF NAMES

Bird groups and the main reference for each are in **bold** letters/numbers. Illustrations are listed in *italics*.
Note: The 'Less Common' species have not been included in this index.